BIRD HAND BOOK

Victor Schrager

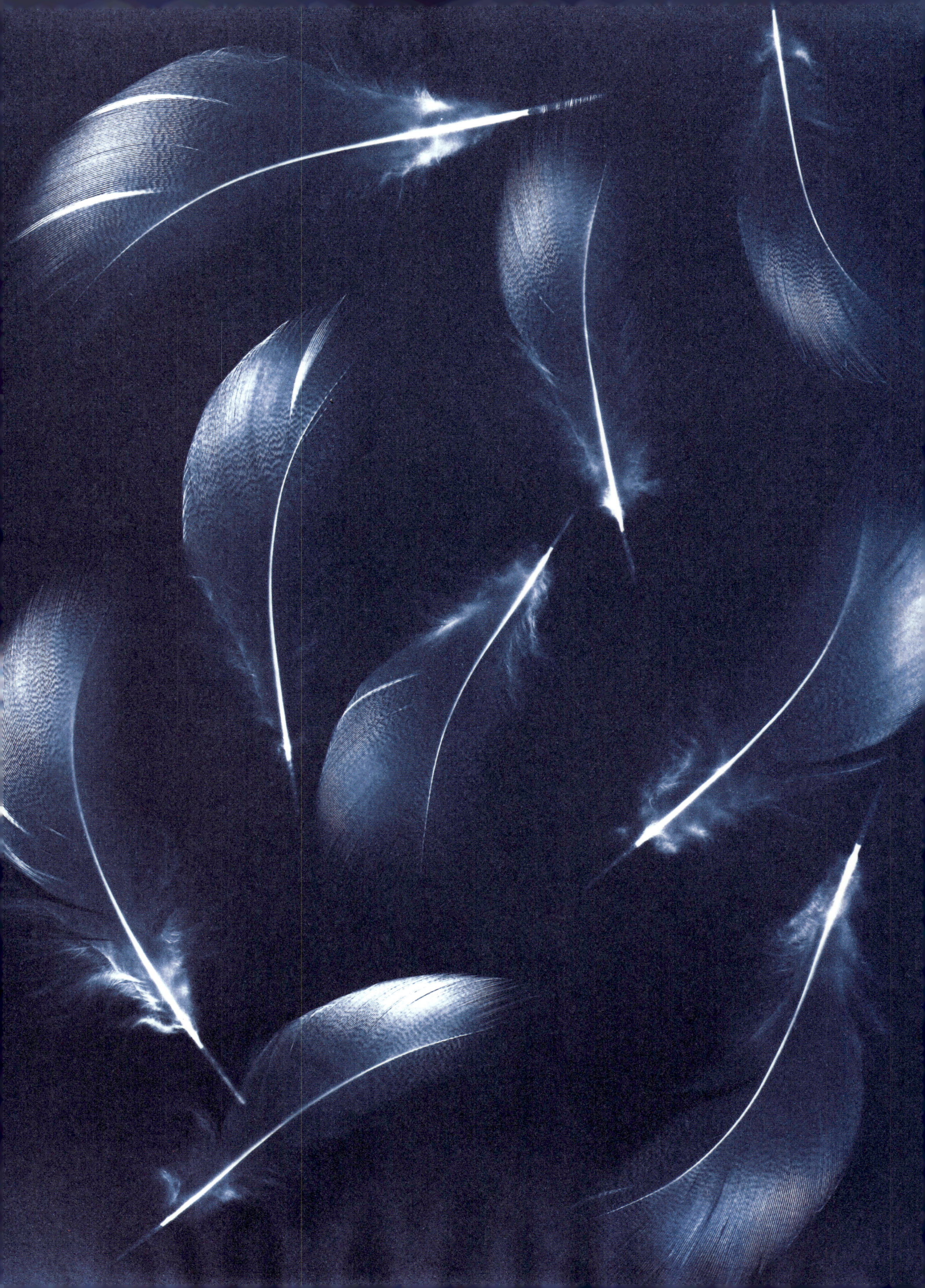

BIRD

PHOTOGRAPHS | VICTOR SCHRAGER

HAND

TEXT | A.S. BYATT

BOOK

DESIGN | DOYLE PARTNERS

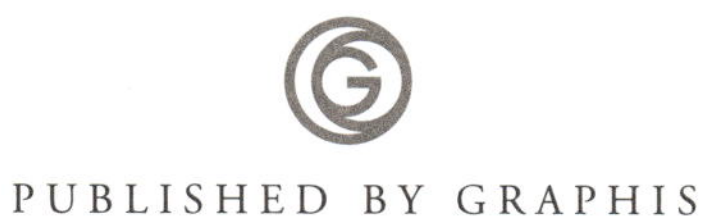

PUBLISHED BY GRAPHIS

307 Fifth Avenue, Tenth Floor
New York, NY 10016.
www.graphis.com

First Edition, 2001
ISBN: 1–931241–04–X

Printed in Hong Kong.

FOR:

A.C.S. M.K.S. V.McC.S.

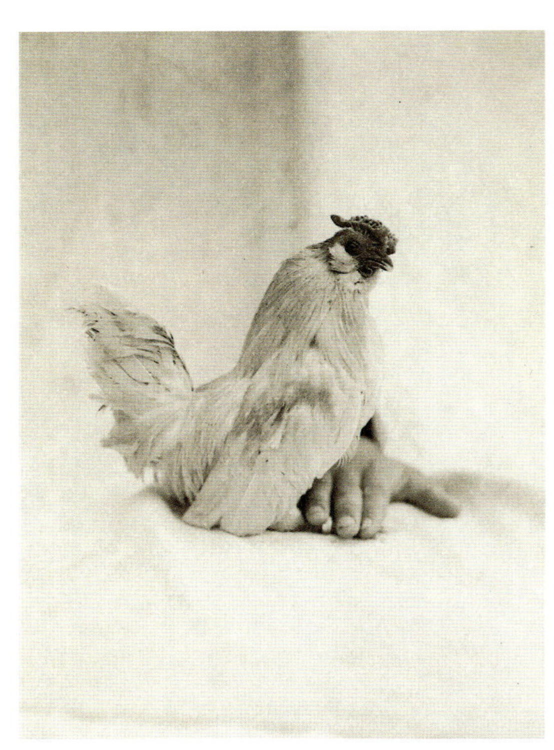

WHITE ROCK CHICKEN

Victor Schrager intrigued me because he said that he wanted to photograph a "list of names." His photographs of birds in the hand say all sorts of things about the relations between birds and humans, but it was the idea of *names* that intrigued me, the language that is the purely human activity.

I love lists—lists as mnemonics, lists as science, lists as poetry. George Eliot, at the seaside in the 1850's with George Henry Lewes and his microscope, wrote, "I never before longed so much to know the names of things as during this visit to Ilfracombe. The desire is part of the tendency that is now growing in me to escape from all vagueness and inaccuracy into the daylight of distinct vivid ideas."

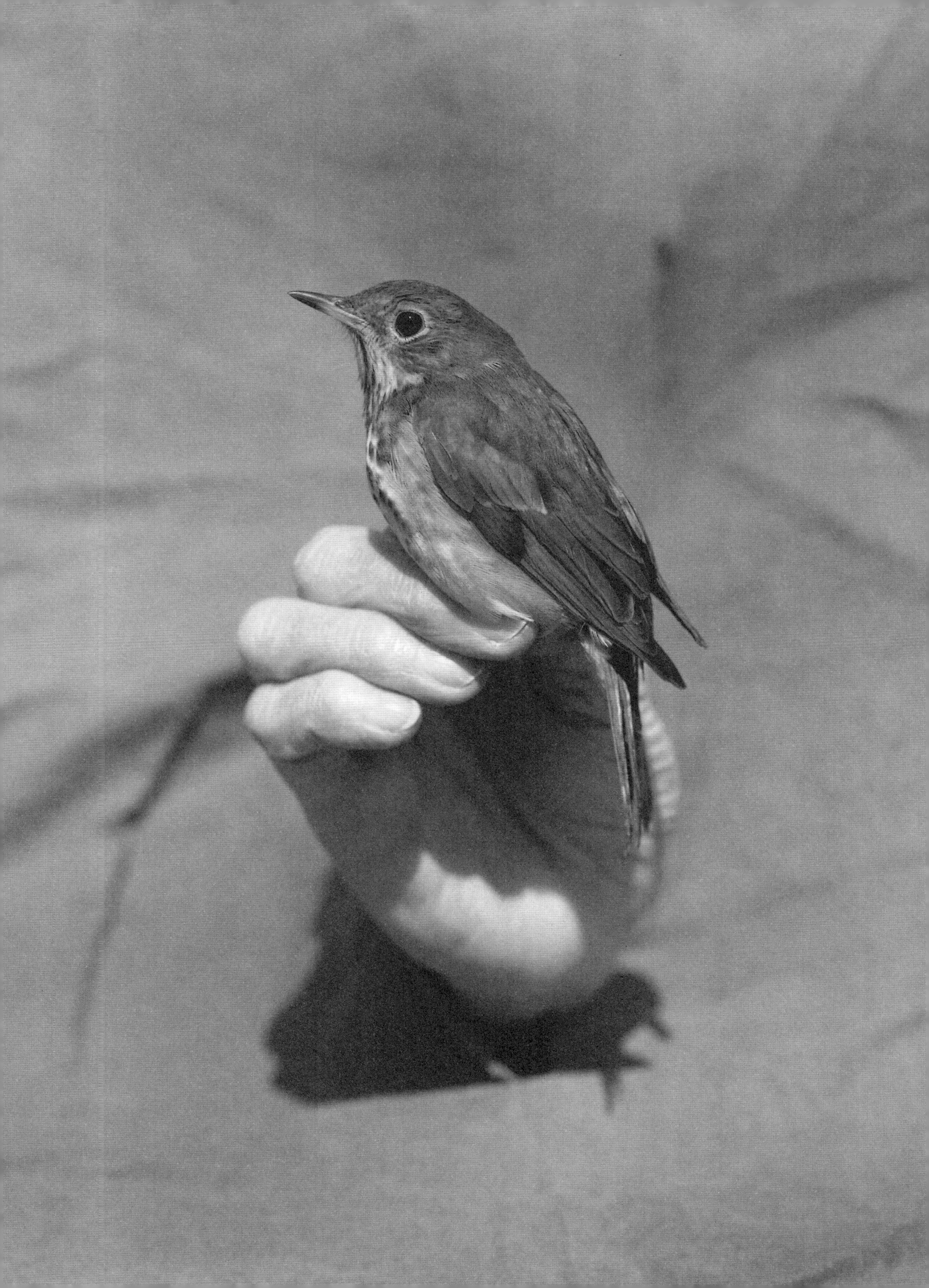

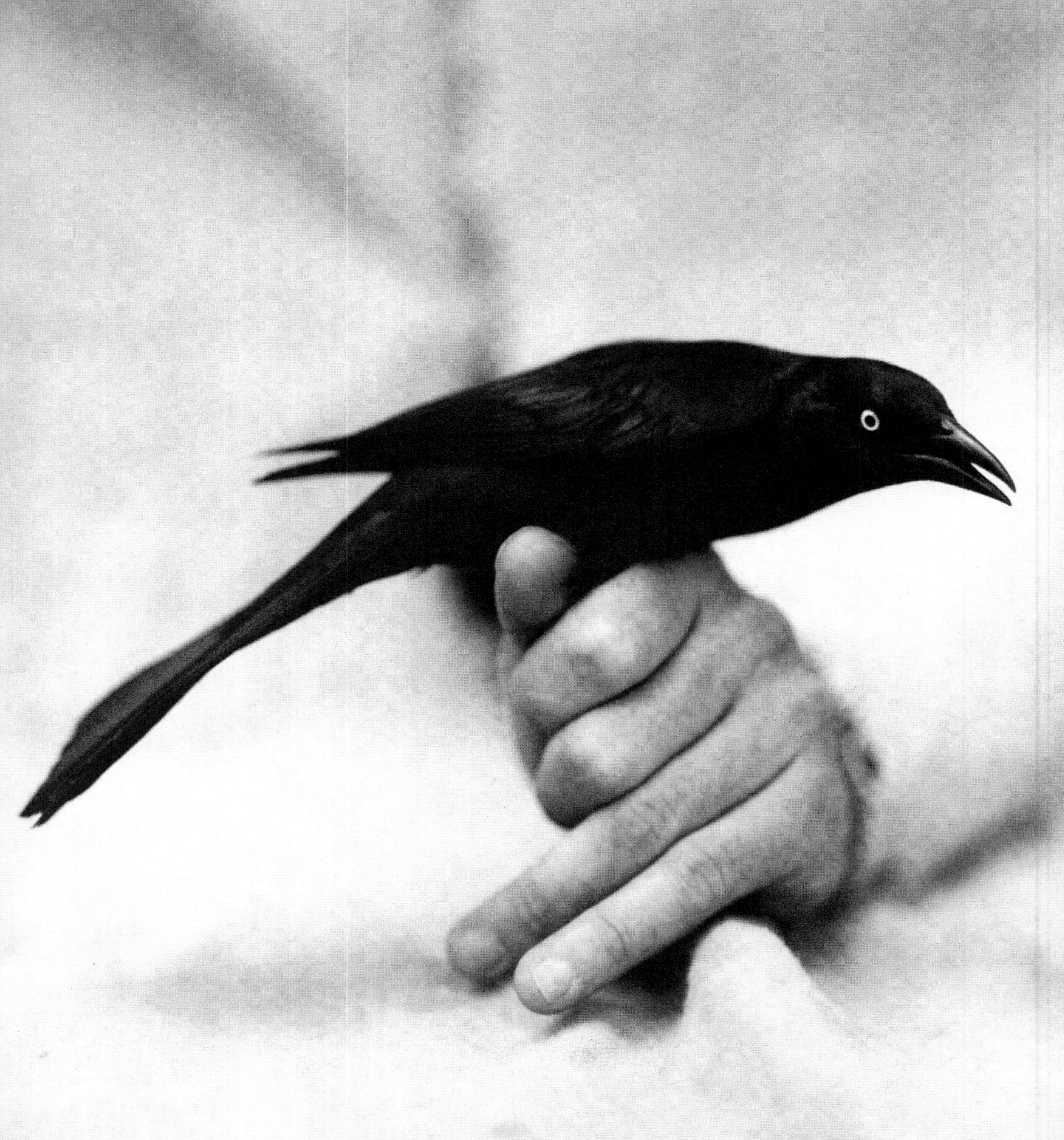

GRACKLE

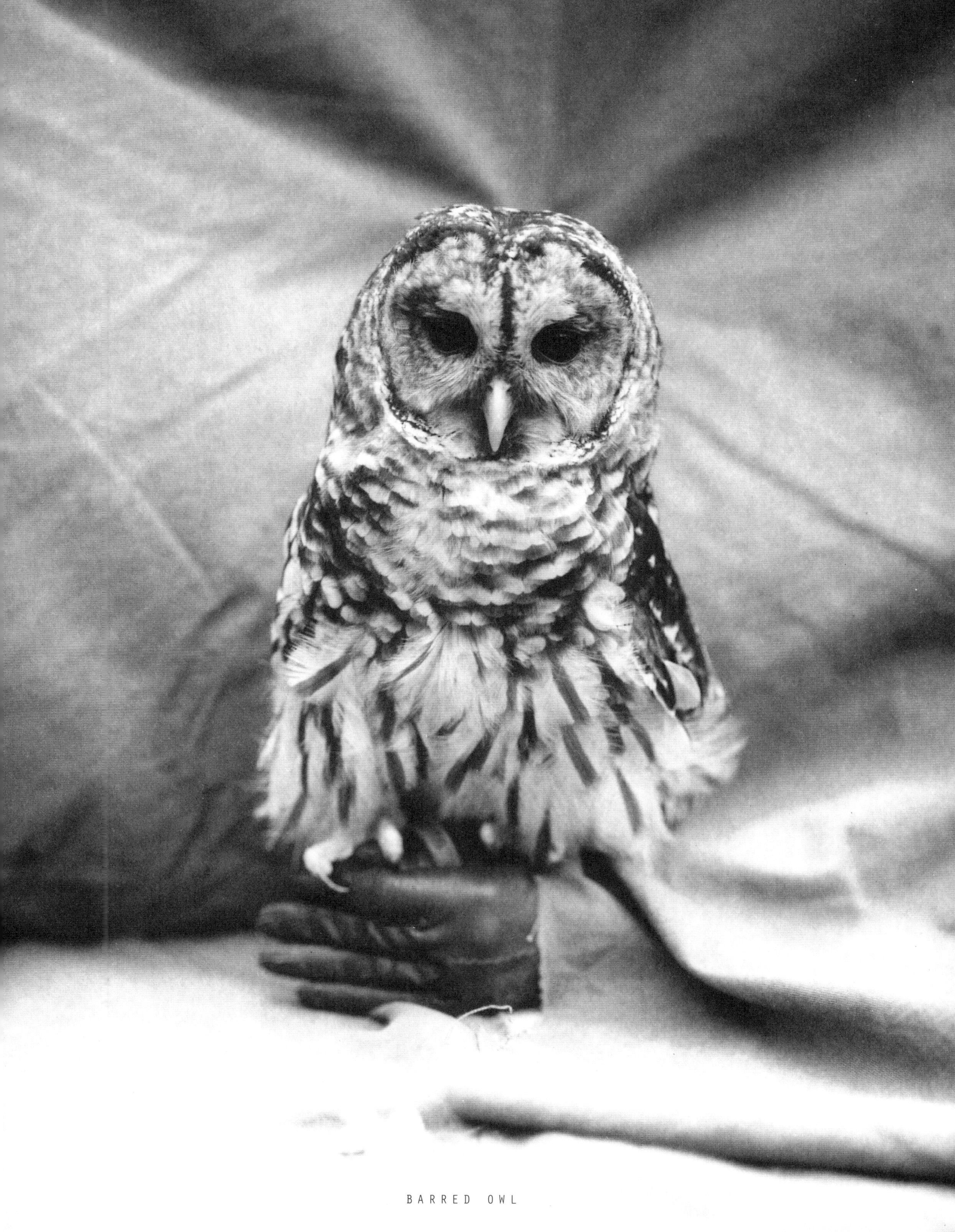

BARRED OWL

Names specify and differentiate; Adam in the garden of Eden created language by naming the creatures. I had the idea of writing a list of lists of birds to go with Victor Schrager's sequence of images, starting with Adam's list. But of course there is a gap between the name and the creature that looks out with bright eyes—the name is a human invention, it is a human attempt to relate to the creatures. I like Robert Frost's sonnet about the distance between human and bird voices in the Garden:

He would declare and could himself believe
That the birds there in all the garden round
From having heard the daylong voice of Eve
Had added to their own an oversound
Her tone of meaning but without the words.
Admittedly an eloquence so soft
Could only have had an influence on birds
When call or laughter carried it aloft.
Be that as may be, she was in their song.
Moreover her voice upon their voices crossed
Had now persisted in the woods so long
That probably it never would be lost.
Never again would birds' song be the same.
And to do that to birds was why she came.

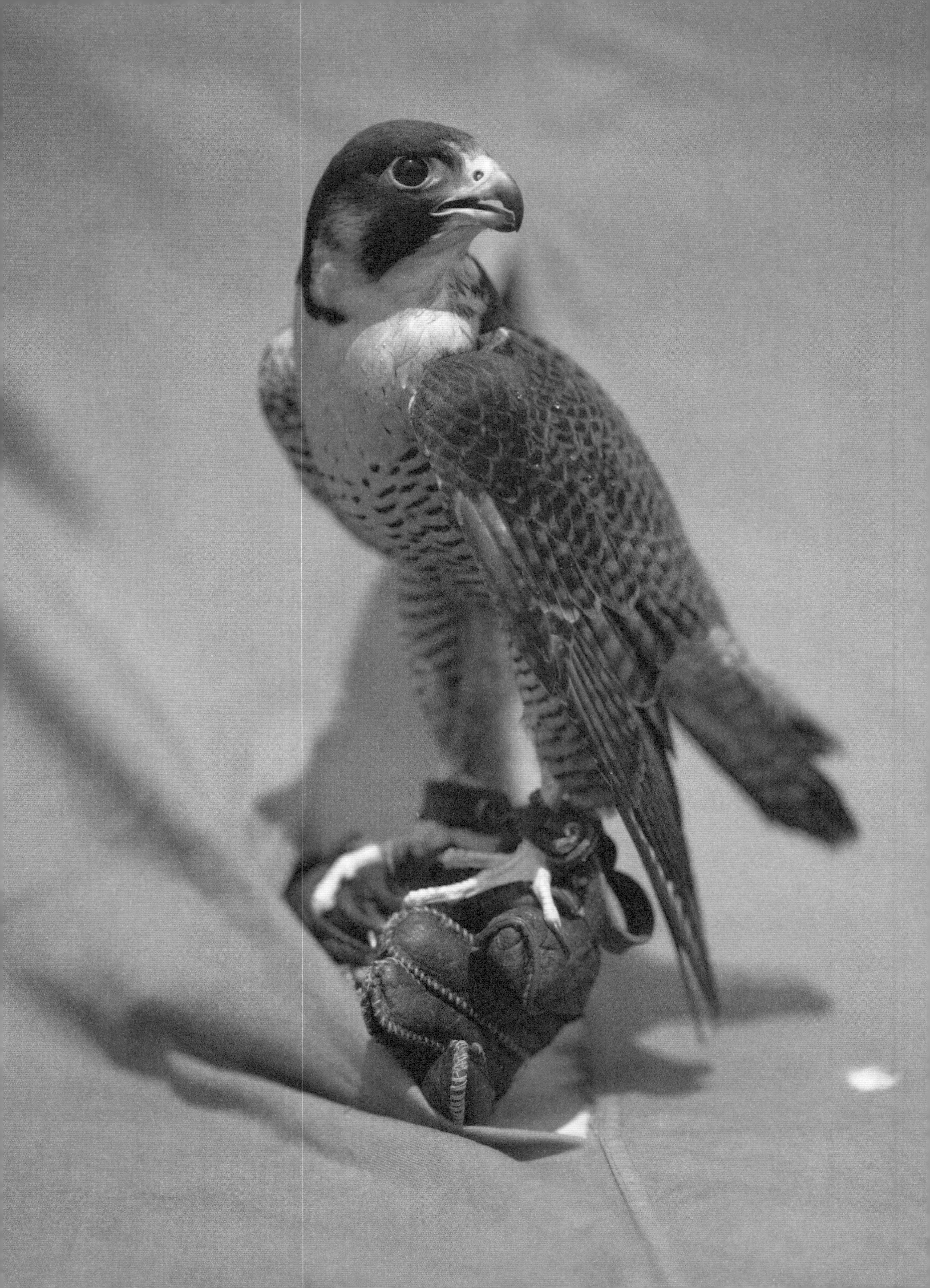

Here is Milton's stately description of the creation of the birds

Mean while the tepid caves, and fens and shores
Their brood as numerous hatch, from the egg that soon
Bursting with kindly rupture forth disclosed
Their callow young, but feathered soon, and fledge
They summed their pens, and soaring the air sublime
With clang despised the ground, under a cloud
In prospect; there the eagle and the stork
On cliffs and cedar tops their eyries build:
Part loosely wing the region, part more wise
In common, ranged in figure wedge their way,
Intelligent of seasons, and set forth
Their airy caravans high over seas
Flying, and over lands with mutual wing
Easing their flight; so steers the prudent crane
Her annual voyage, borne on winds; the air
Floats, as they pass, fanned with unnumbered plumes:
From branch to branch the smaller birds with song
Solaced the woods, and spread their painted wings
Till even, nor then the solemn nightingale
Ceased warbling, but all night tuned her soft lays:
Others on silver lakes and rivers bathed
Their downy breast; the swan with arched neck
Between her white wings mantling proudly, rows
Her state with oary feet: yet oft they quit
The dank, and rising on stiff pennons tower
The mid aerial sky: others on ground
Walked firm; the crested cock whose clarion sounds
The silent hours, and the other whose gay train
Adorns him, coloured with the florid hue
Of rainbow and starry eyes.

[Paradise Lost VII 417–446]

Milton's list is short and he does not *name* the peacock at all, making the bird a mystery of flowery and starry colours and eyes. His birds are reminiscent of the carefully observed and painted birds of Brueghel's Paradise gardens. *Paradise Lost* looks forwards and backwards—Milton's birds are both clearly observed (note the beautiful verb "wedge" in the clear description of migrating flocks) and full of symbolic importance; his list starts with the conventional king of birds and moves through those whose emblematic significance was well-known. The stork and the crane typified military discipline and prudence, the nightingale and the swan purity, music, and poetry. Medieval bestiaries deploy these symbolic relations between birds and men. In 1954 T.H. White made a vigorous translation of a twelfth-century one, which included the mythic phoenix and the singing sirens amongst the birds, along with an unidentified bird called the Caladrius, which was completely white without a speck of black. Its dung, we are told, is good for eye-trouble, and if it turns its back on a sick man it is an infallible sign that he will die. White's best bird *list* is one of names invented in mimicry of the birds' voices:

"Grus,
Corvus,
Cignus,
Bubo,
Milvus,
Ulula,
Cuculus,
Garrulus,
Graculus,
etc.
(Crane,
Crow,
Swan,
Owl, Kite,
Screech-
Owl,
Cuckoo
Starling,
Daw.)"

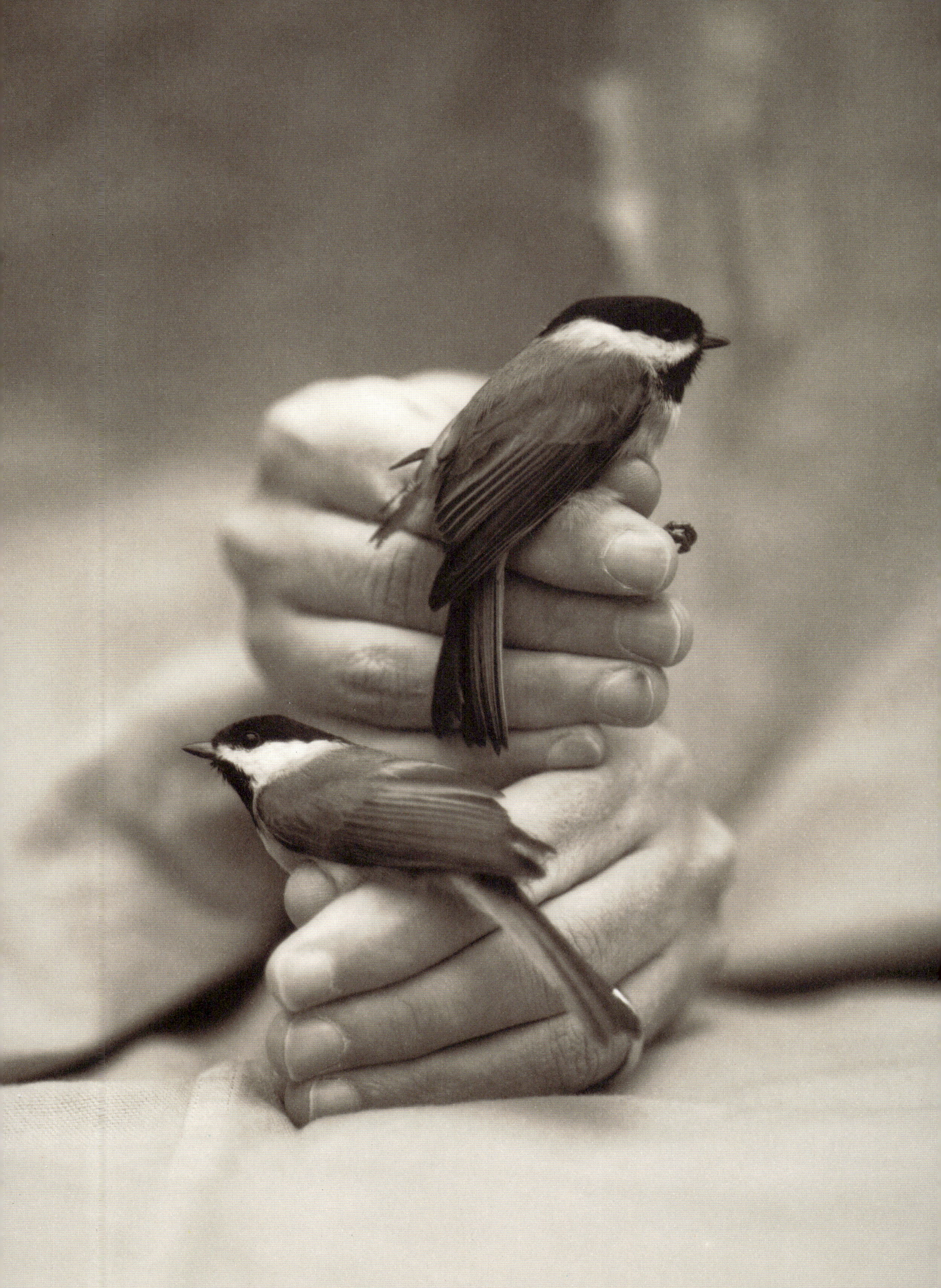

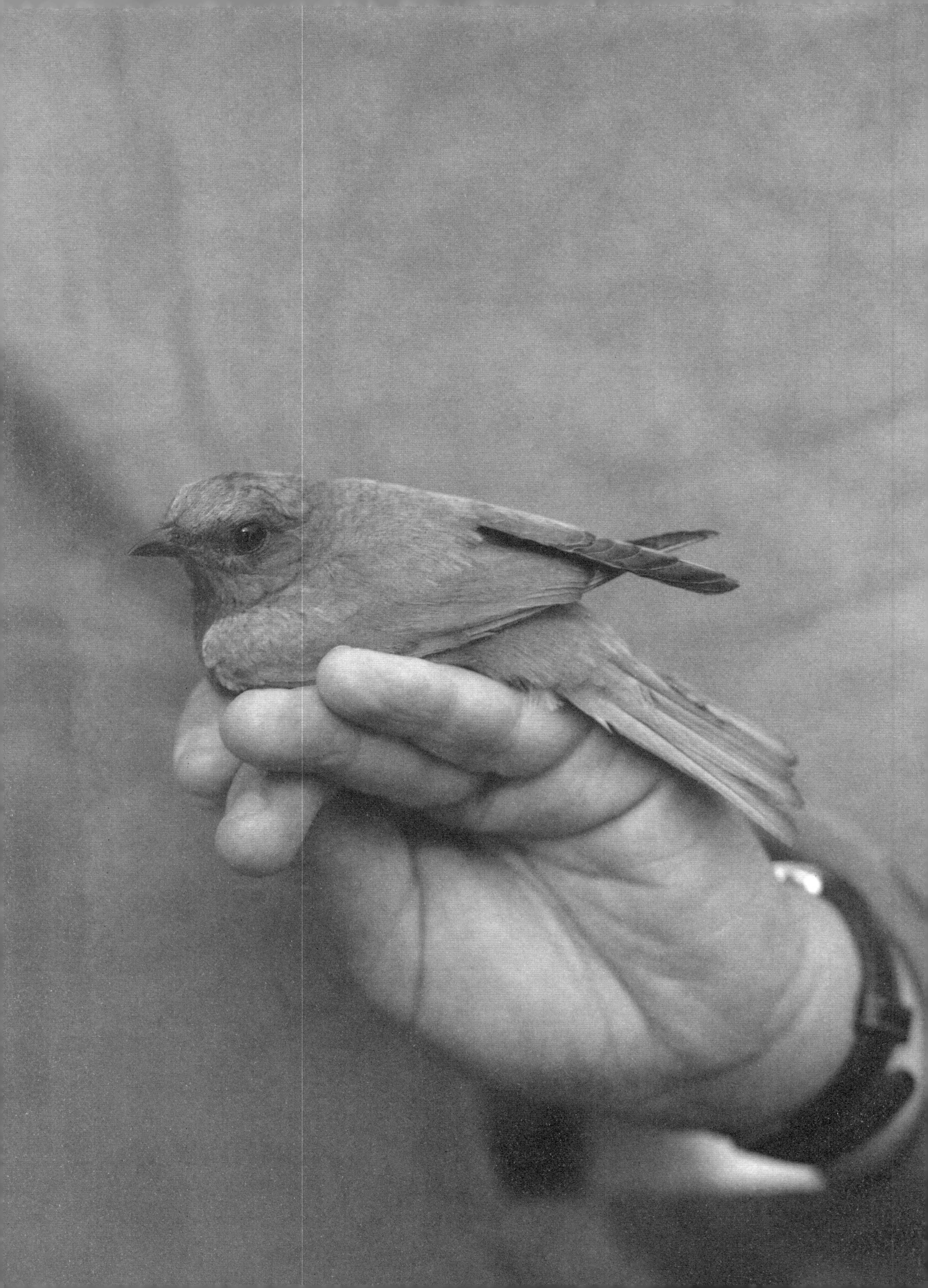

He points out that, "Why did the owl 'owl is an accurate piece of etymology. Its name in most languages is of echoic origin." The entry on Columba the Dove is a list of another kind, alas too long to quote in its entirety, of analogies between the Dove and Preachers. "Columba the Dove is a simple fowl and free from gall, and it asks for love with its eye. (In the same way, Preachers are free from gall or acrimoniousness, because although they may be in a rage, it is not to be called anger when they are exasperated with good reason.) The dove has groan instead of a song. (Thus Preachers, being far from provocative songs and from the fashion of the times, groan over the sins of themselves and others.) Nor does this bird mangle things with its beak, and this fact well applies to Preachers, who do not falsify the sacred scriptures as heretics do. The dove picks out the better grains: the Preacher chooses the better maxims from holy writ.... The bird sits near streams so that on seeing a hawk it can dive in and escape: similarly the Preachers live near the blessed scriptures so that, on seeing an attack and temptation from the devil they can dive into the scriptures...and so escape."

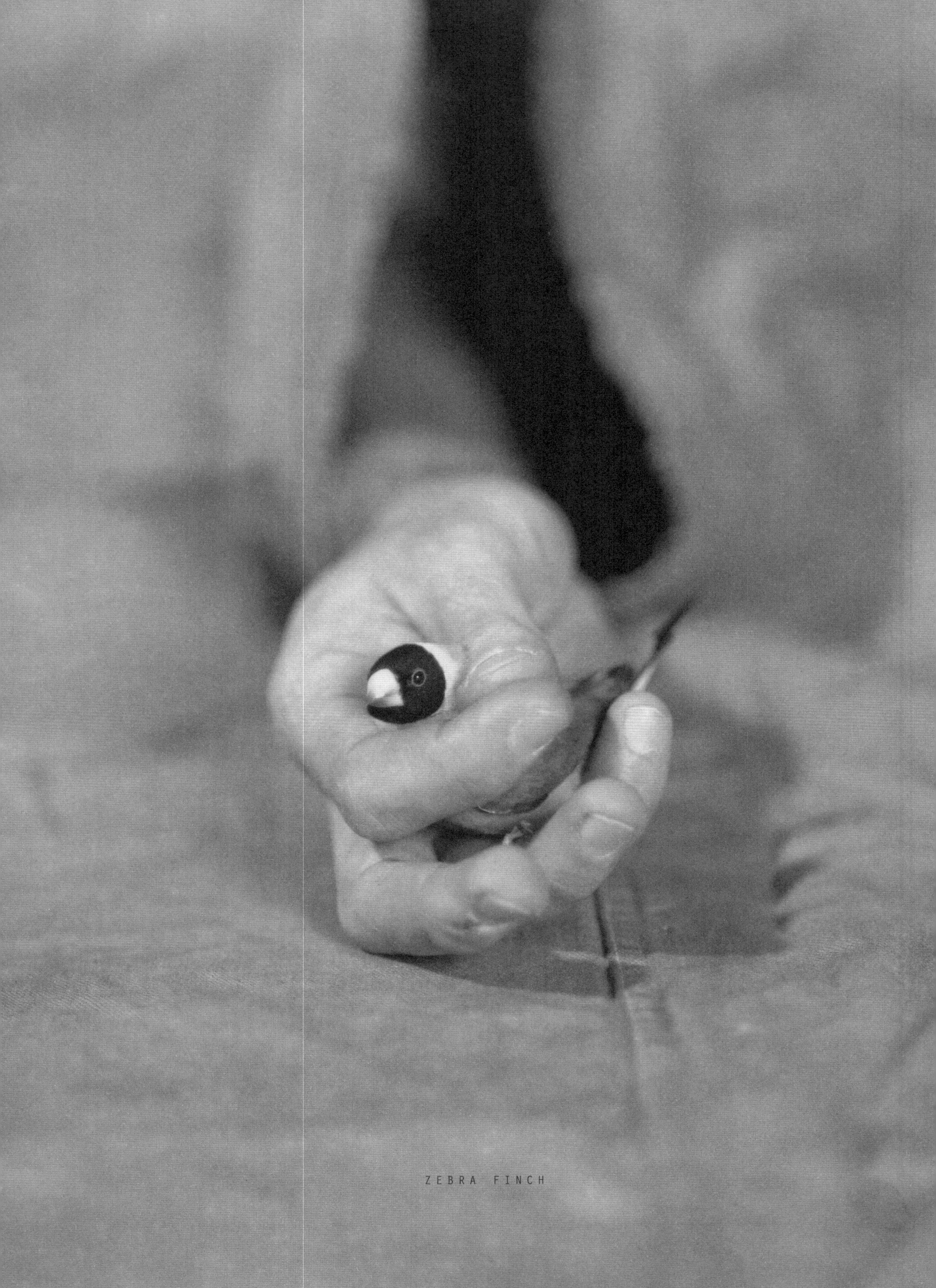

ZEBRA FINCH

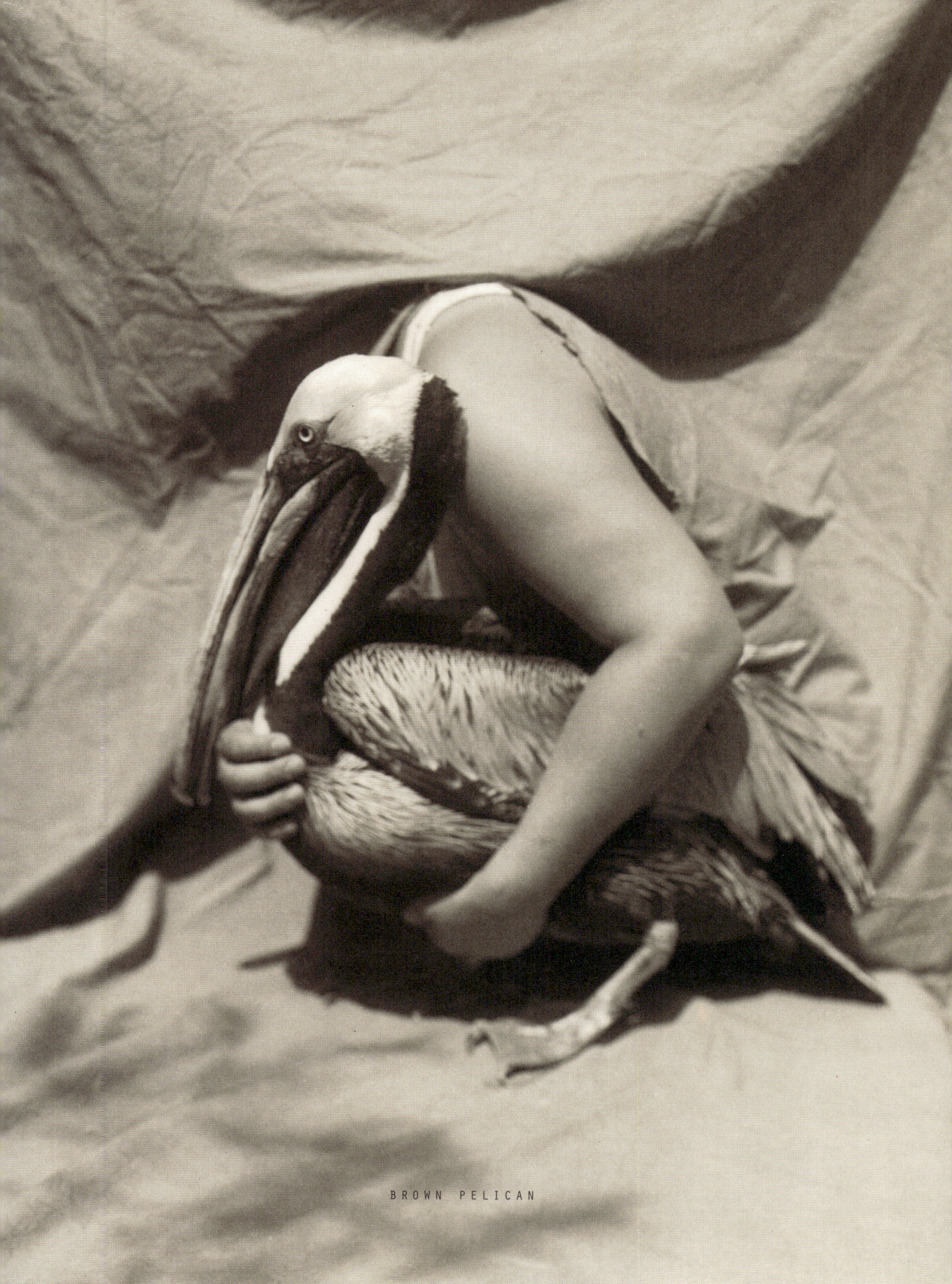

BROWN PELICAN

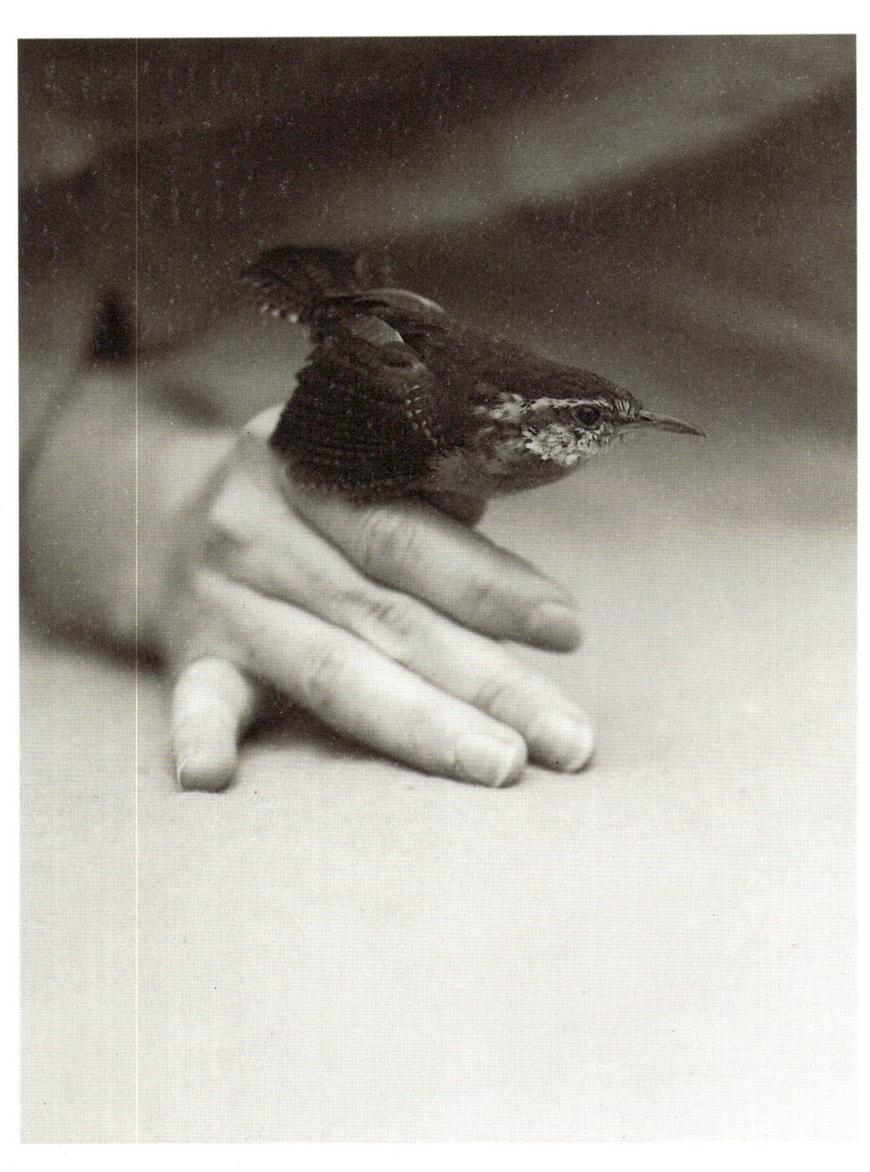

CAROLINA WREN

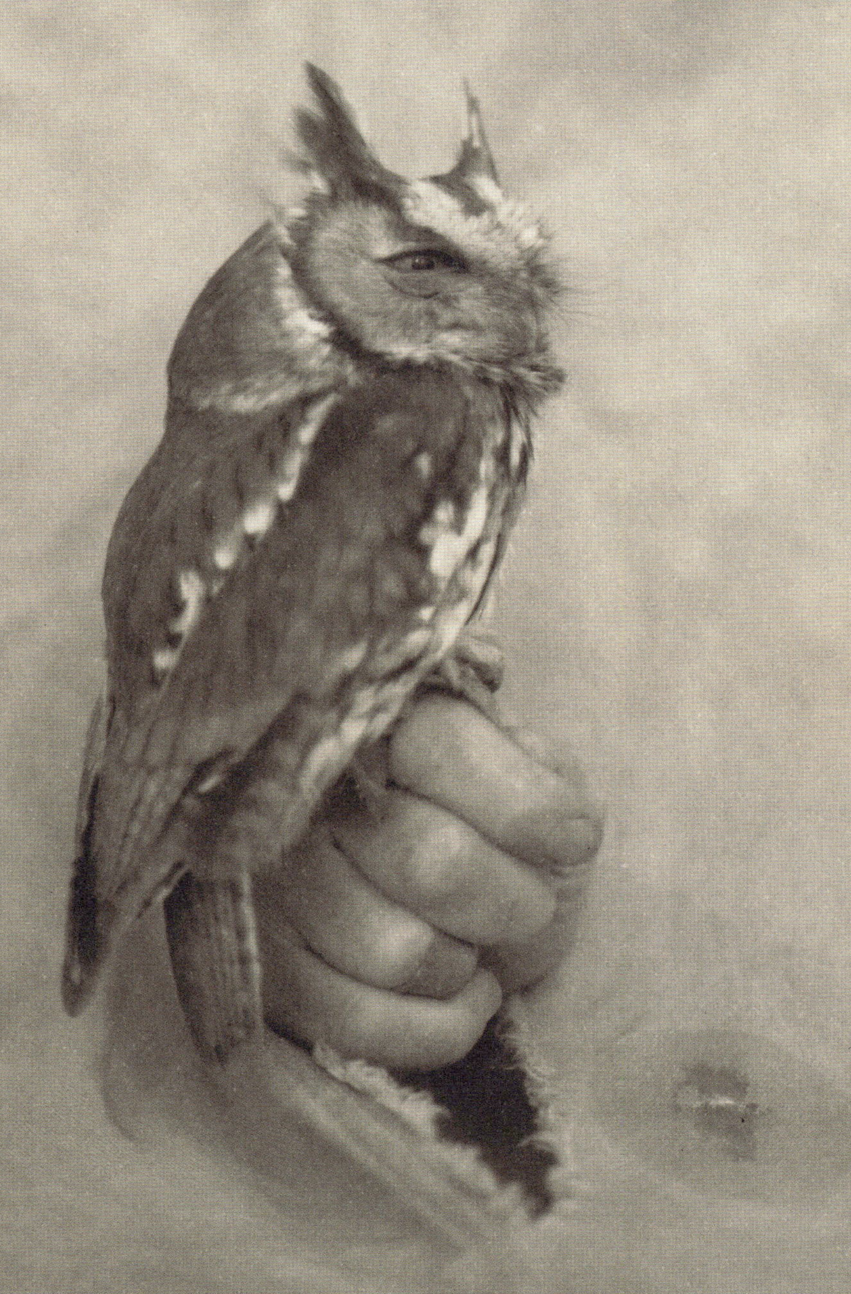

SCREECH OWL

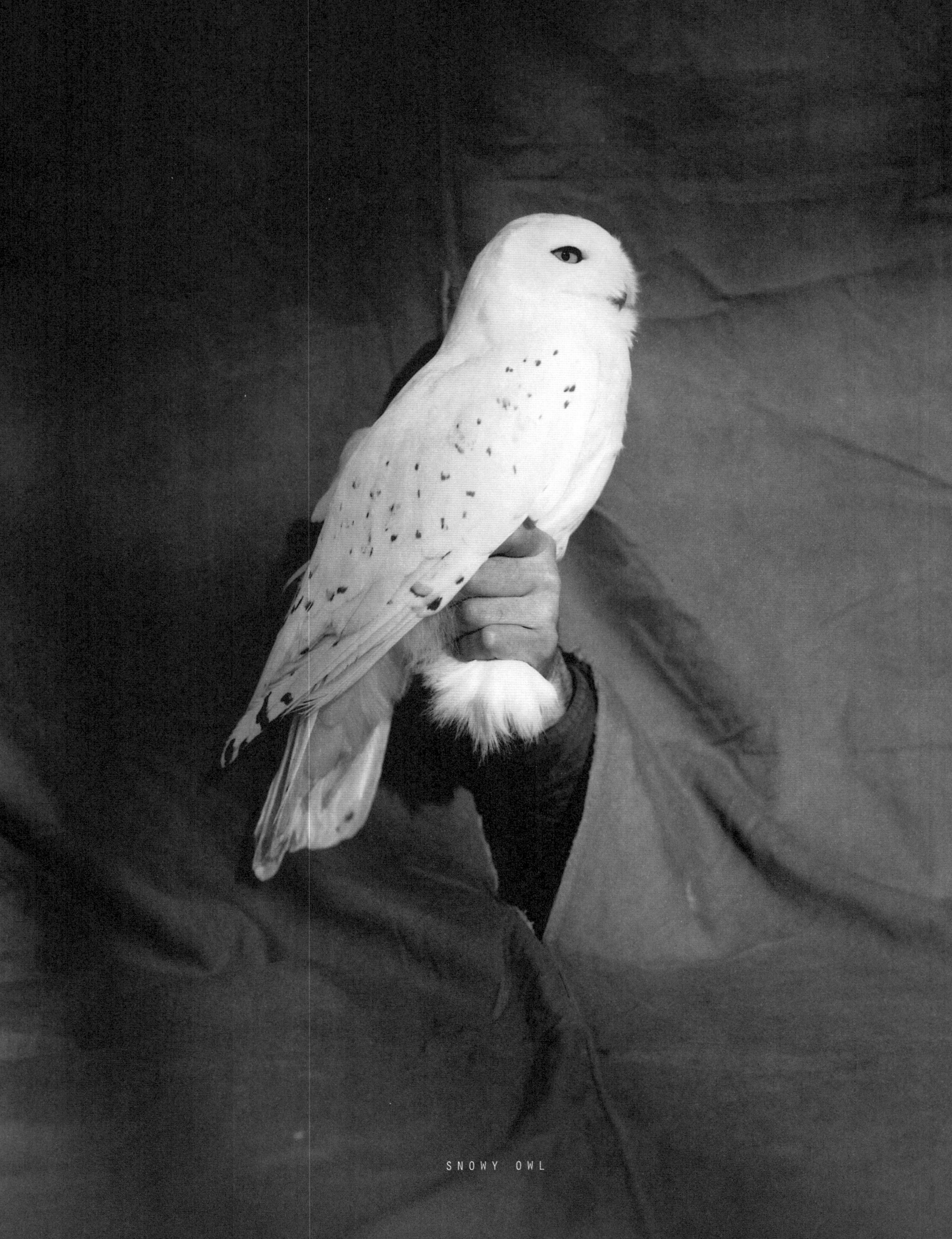

SNOWY OWL

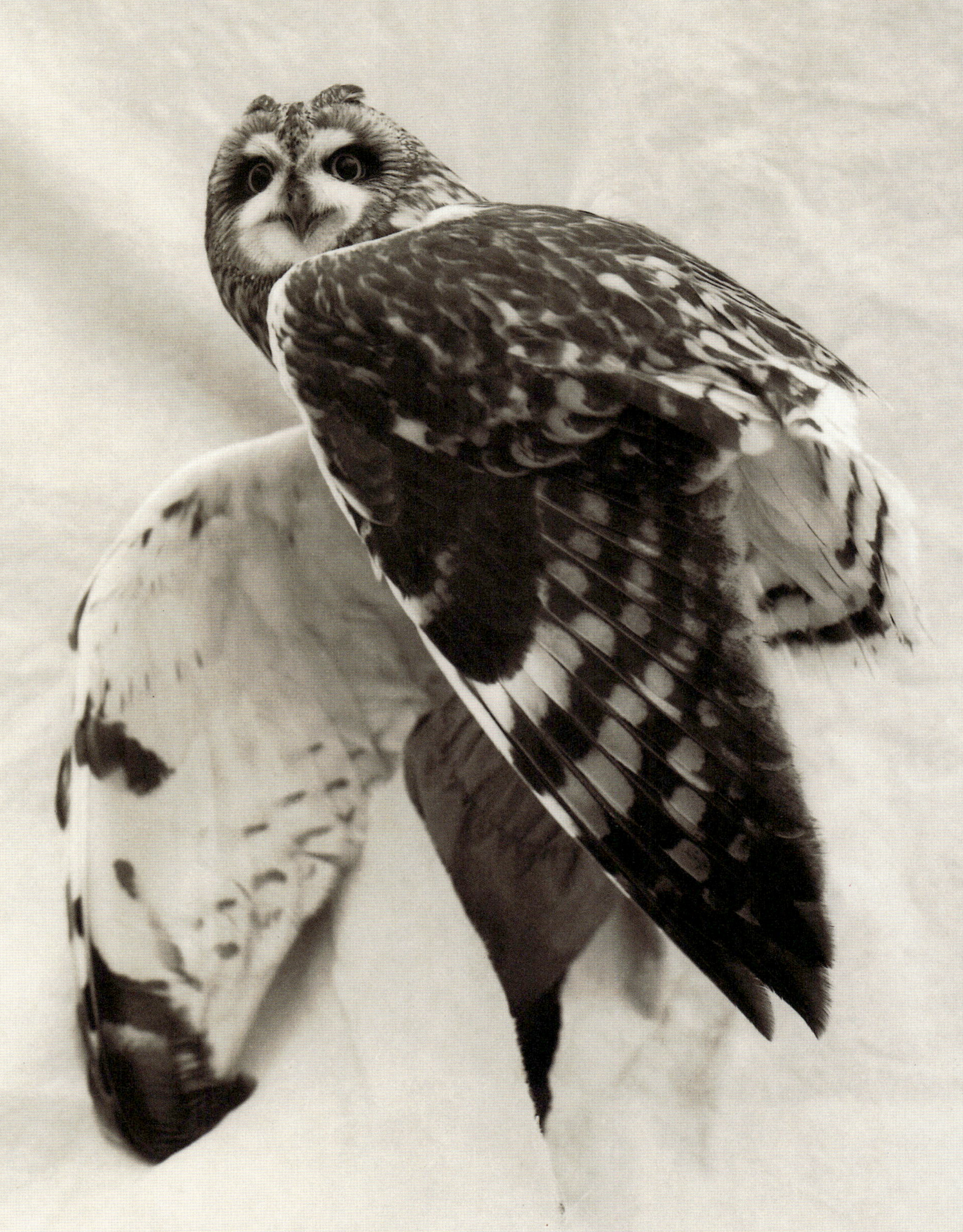

SHORT-EARED OWL

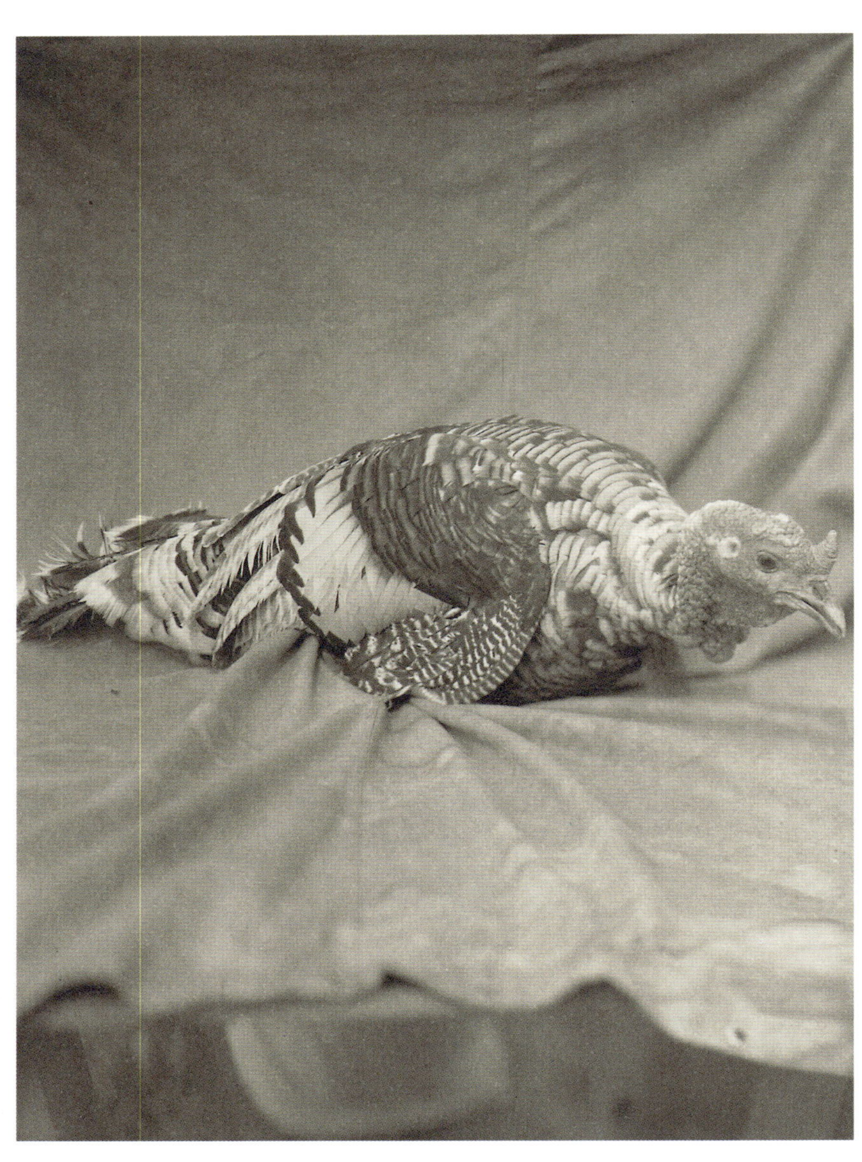

BRONZE TURKEY

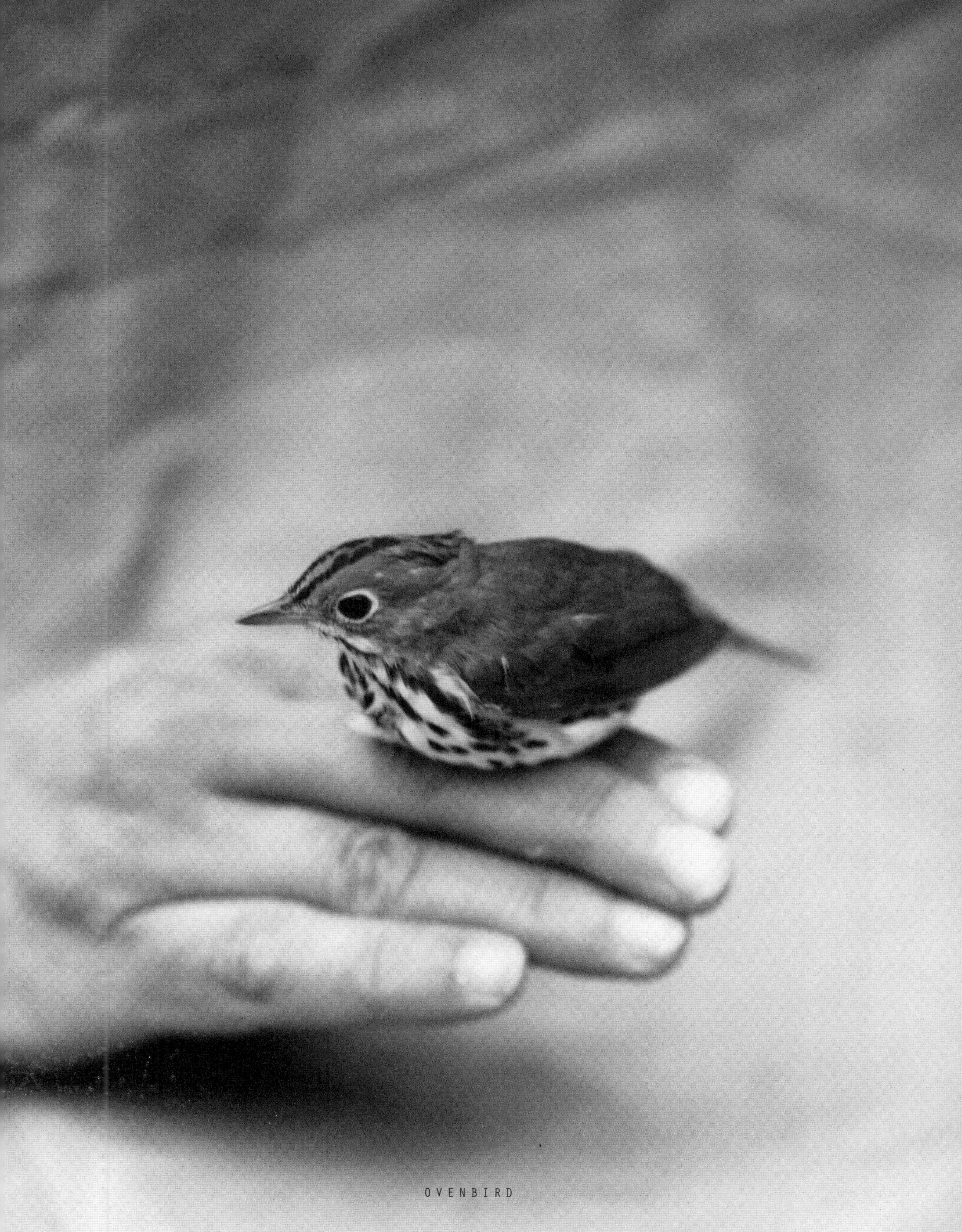

OVENBIRD

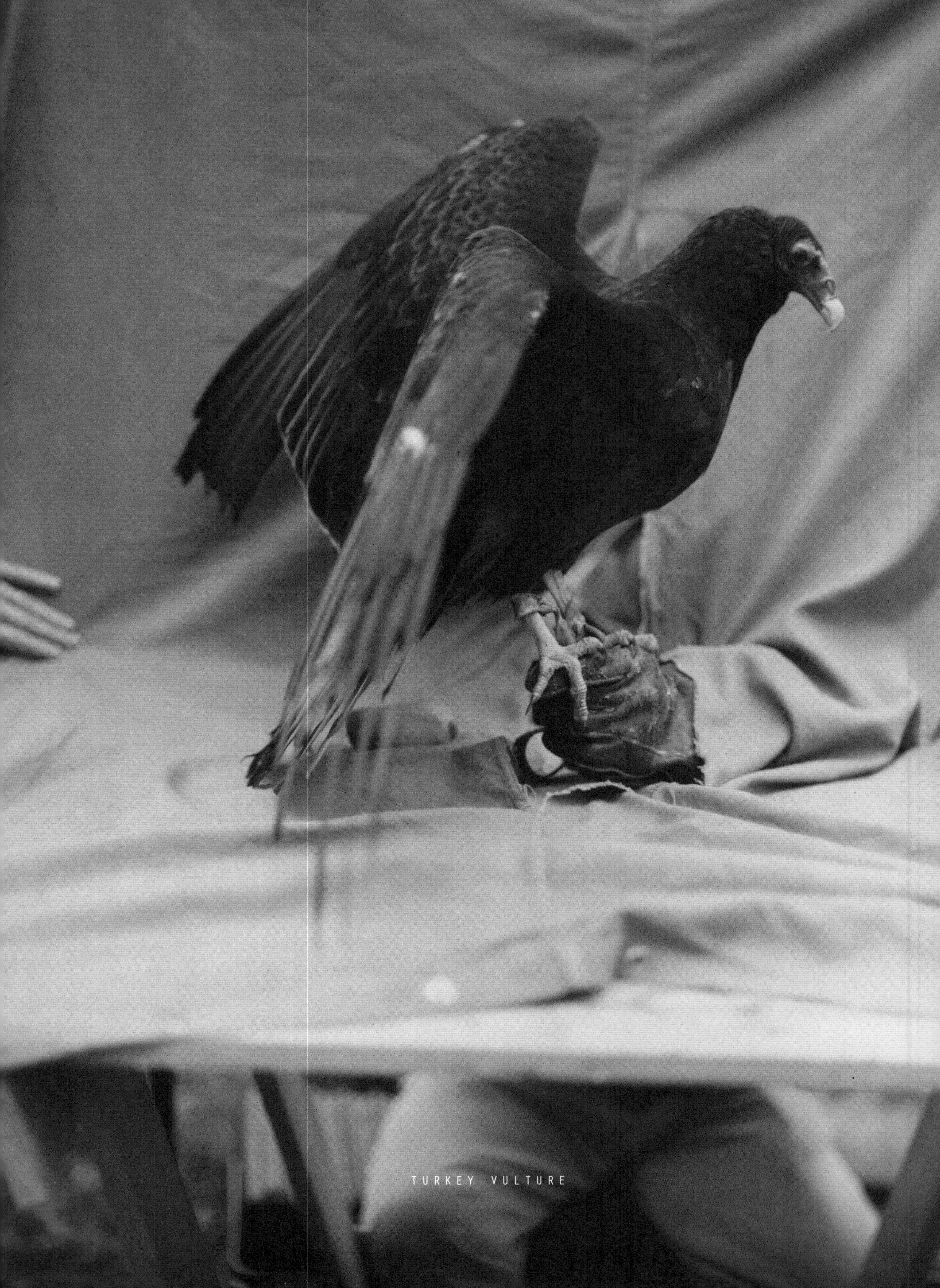

TURKEY VULTURE

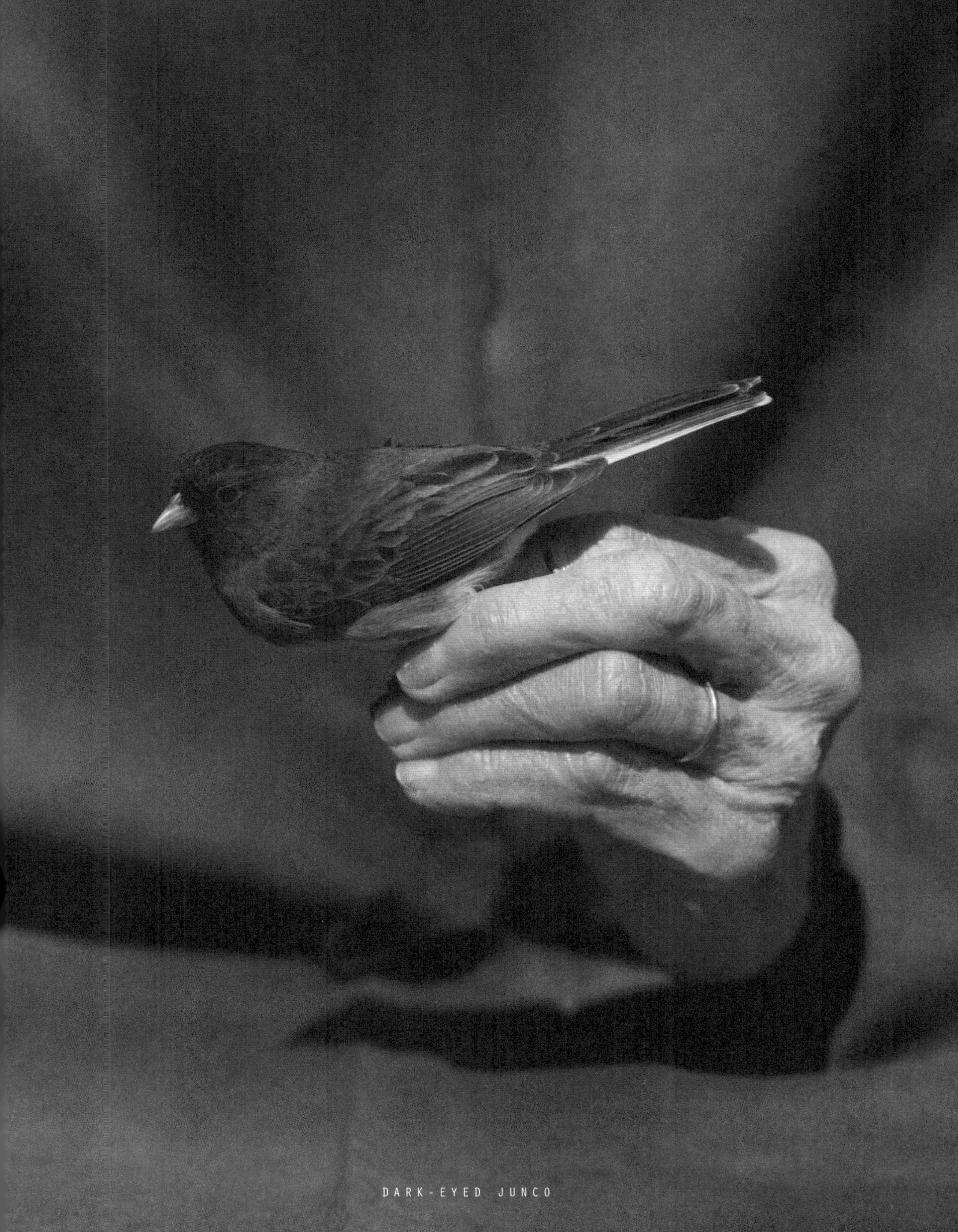

DARK-EYED JUNCO

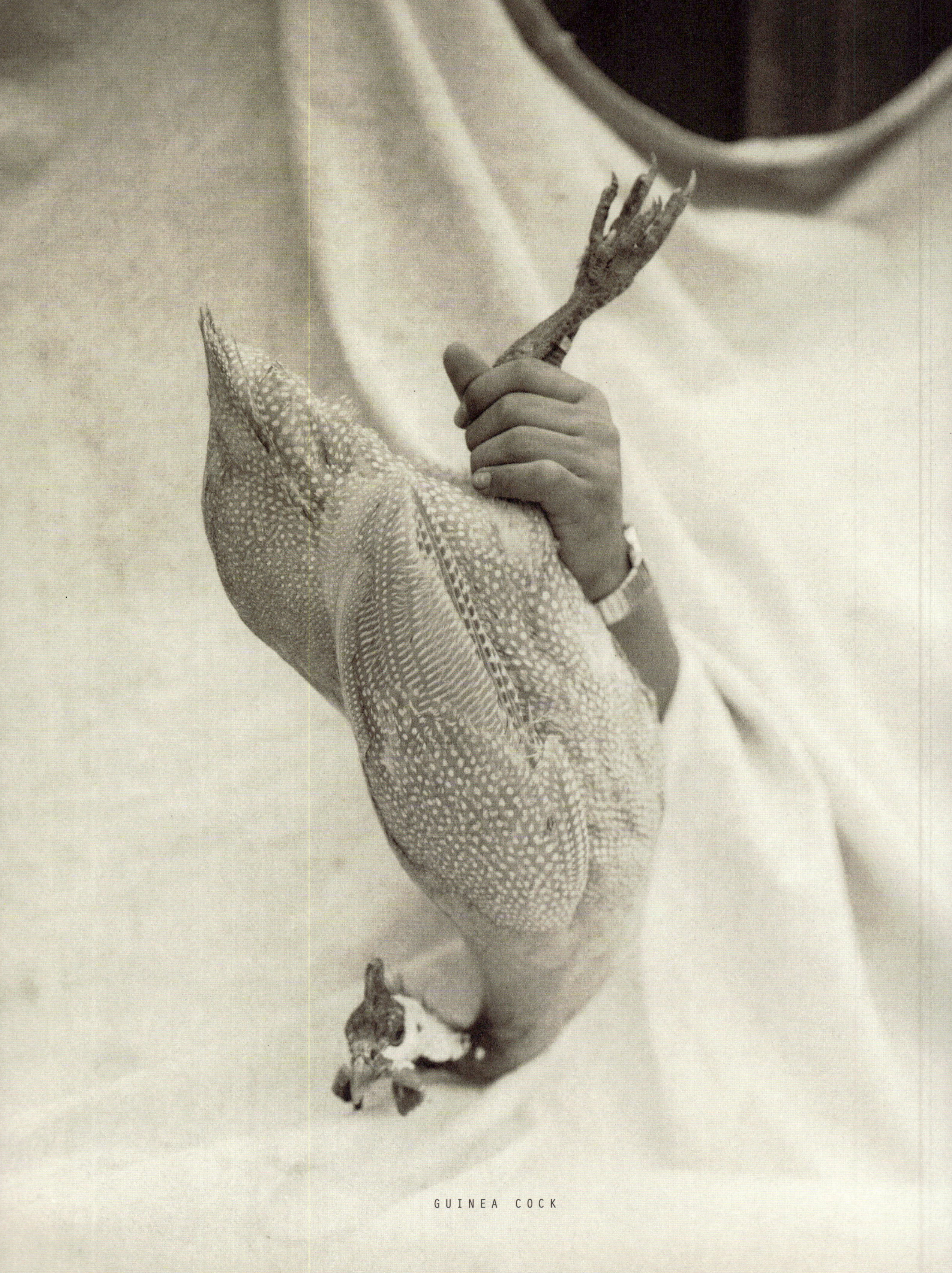

GUINEA COCK

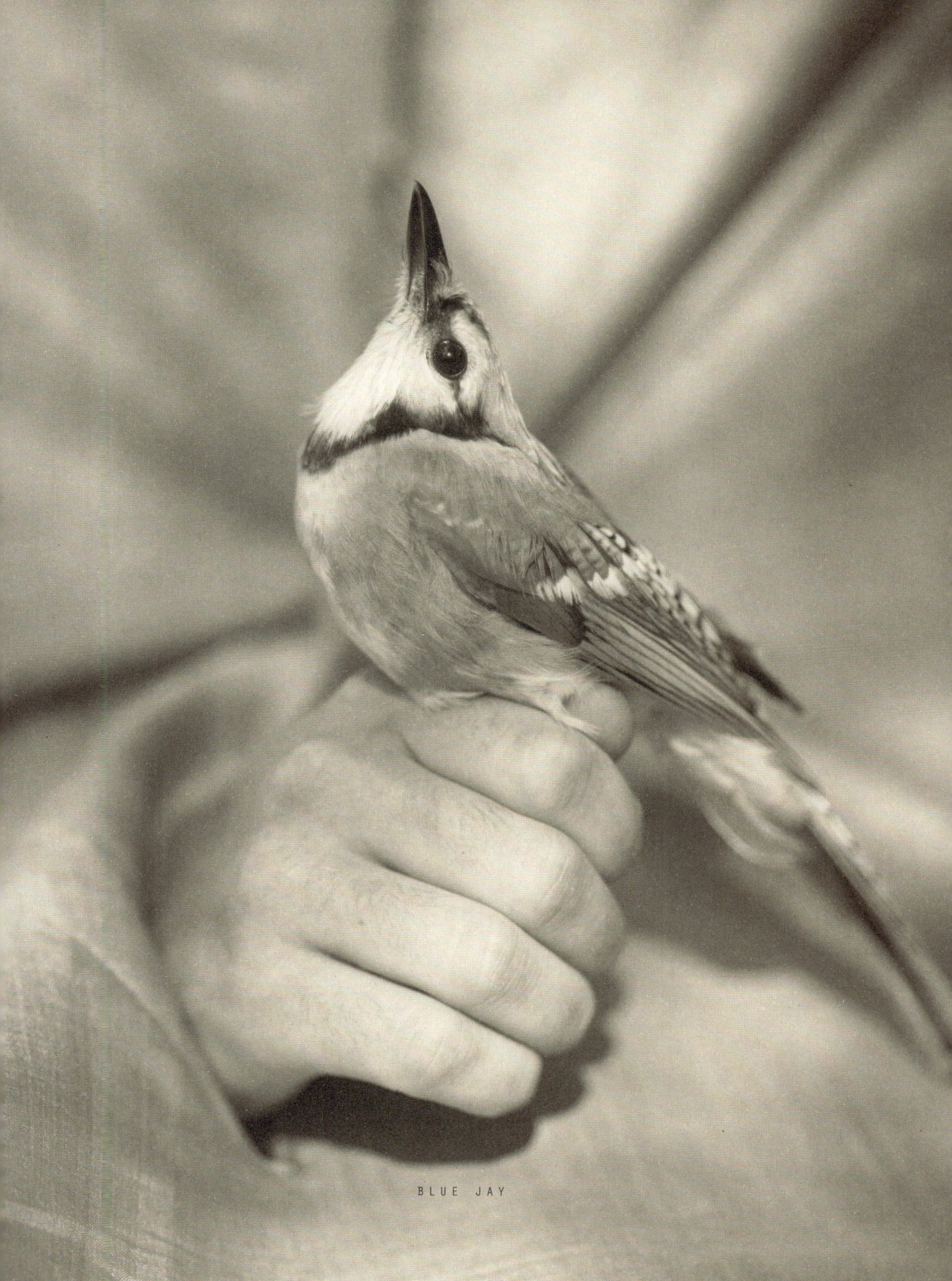

BLUE JAY

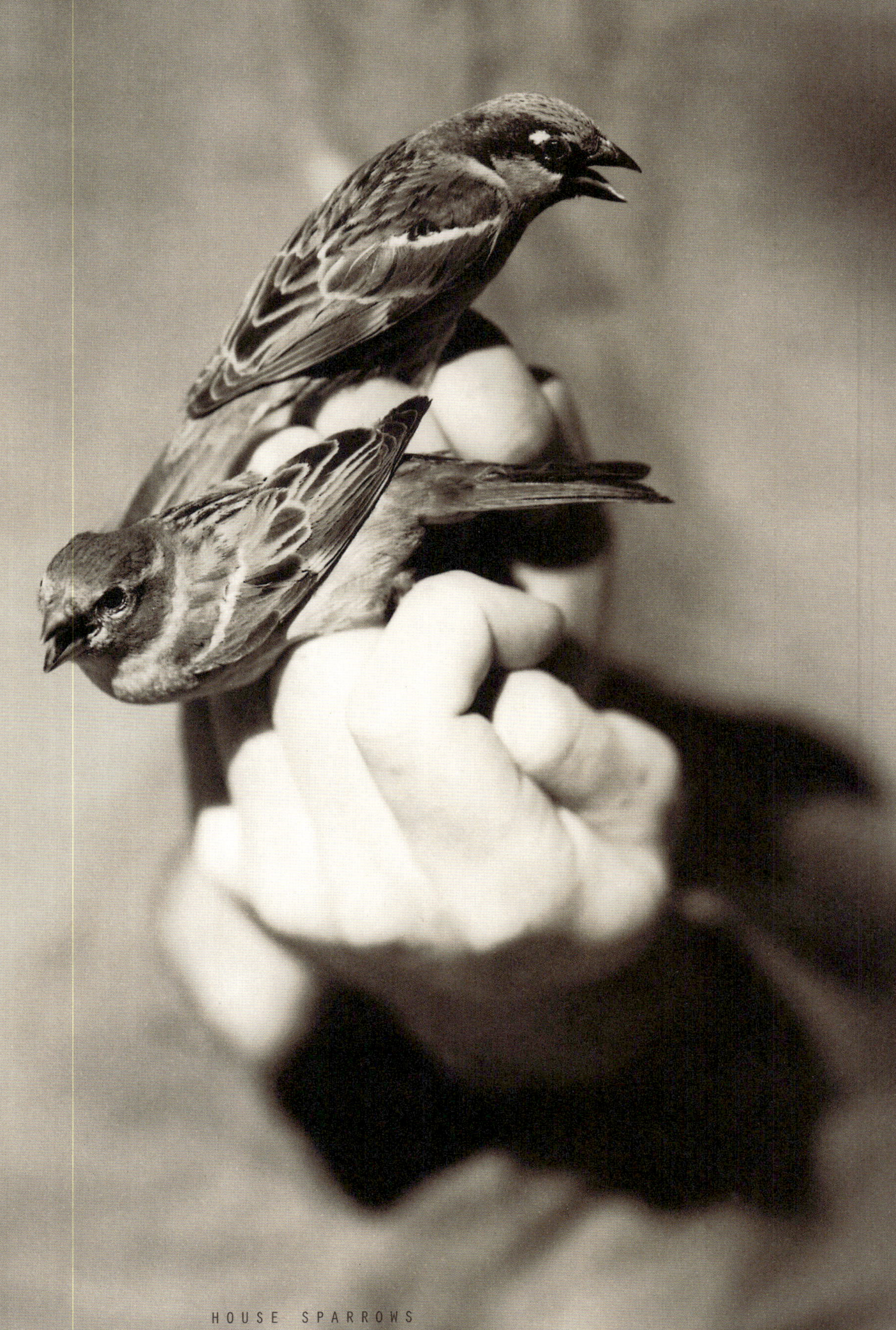

HOUSE SPARROWS

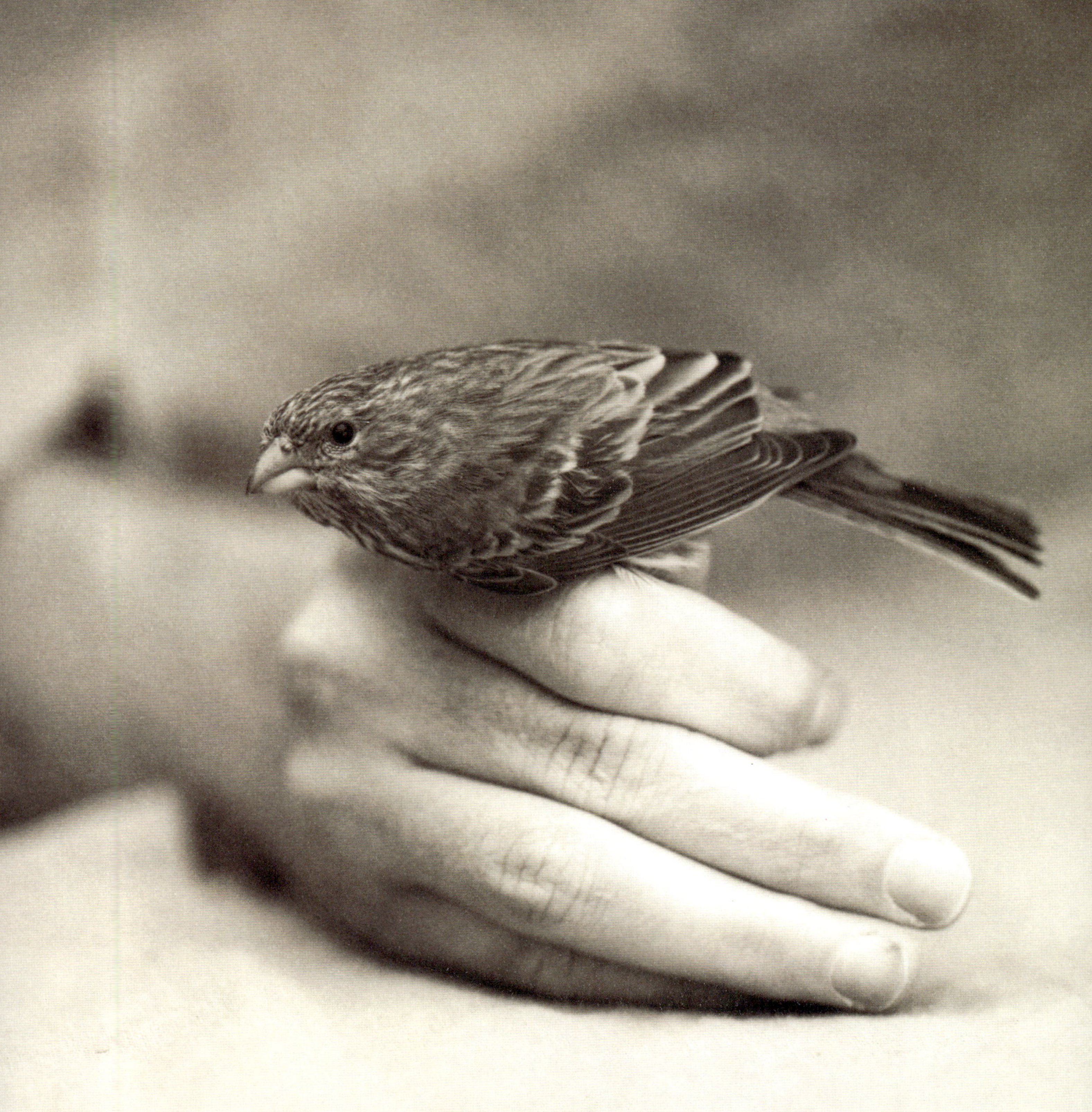

HOUSE FINCH

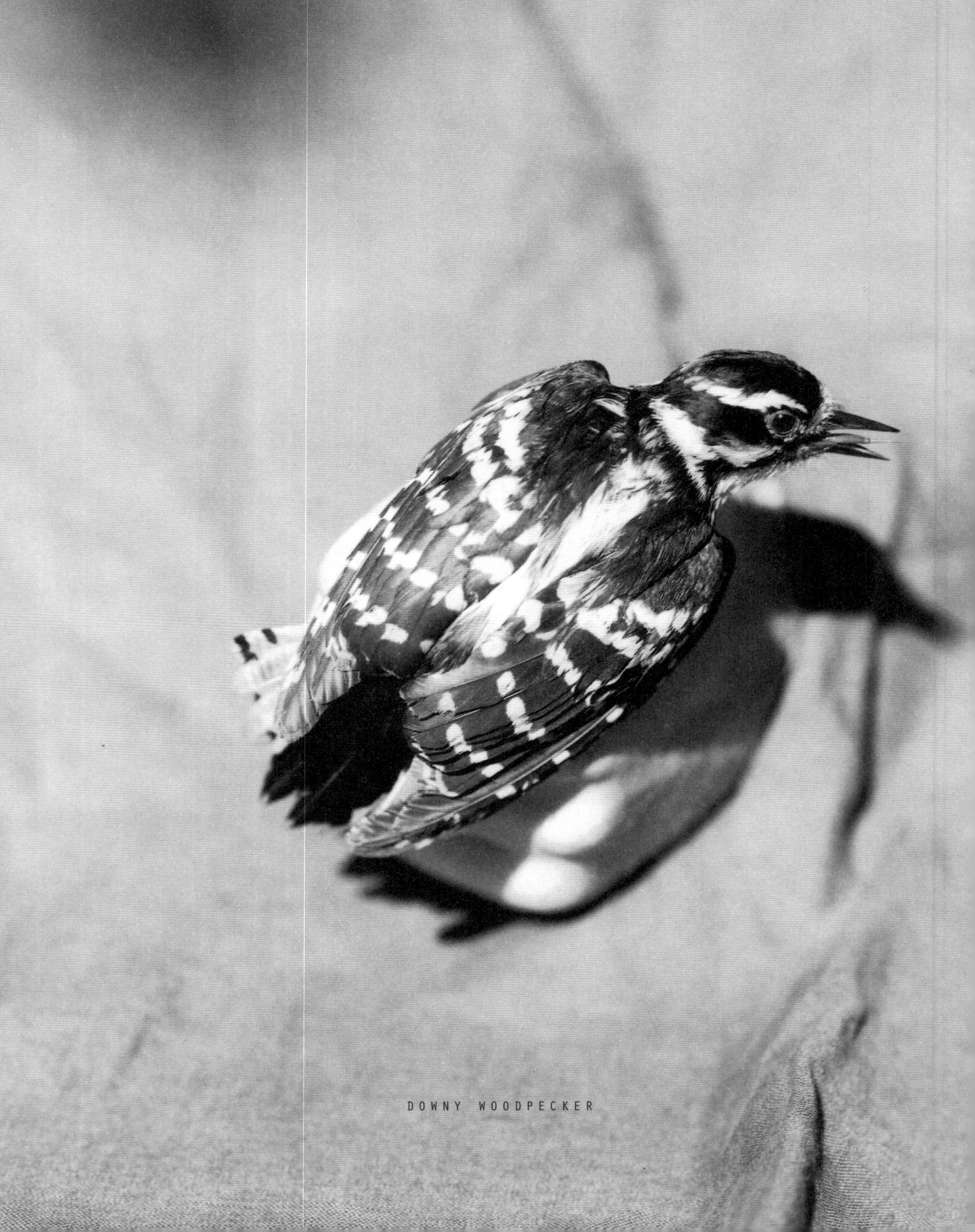

DOWNY WOODPECKER

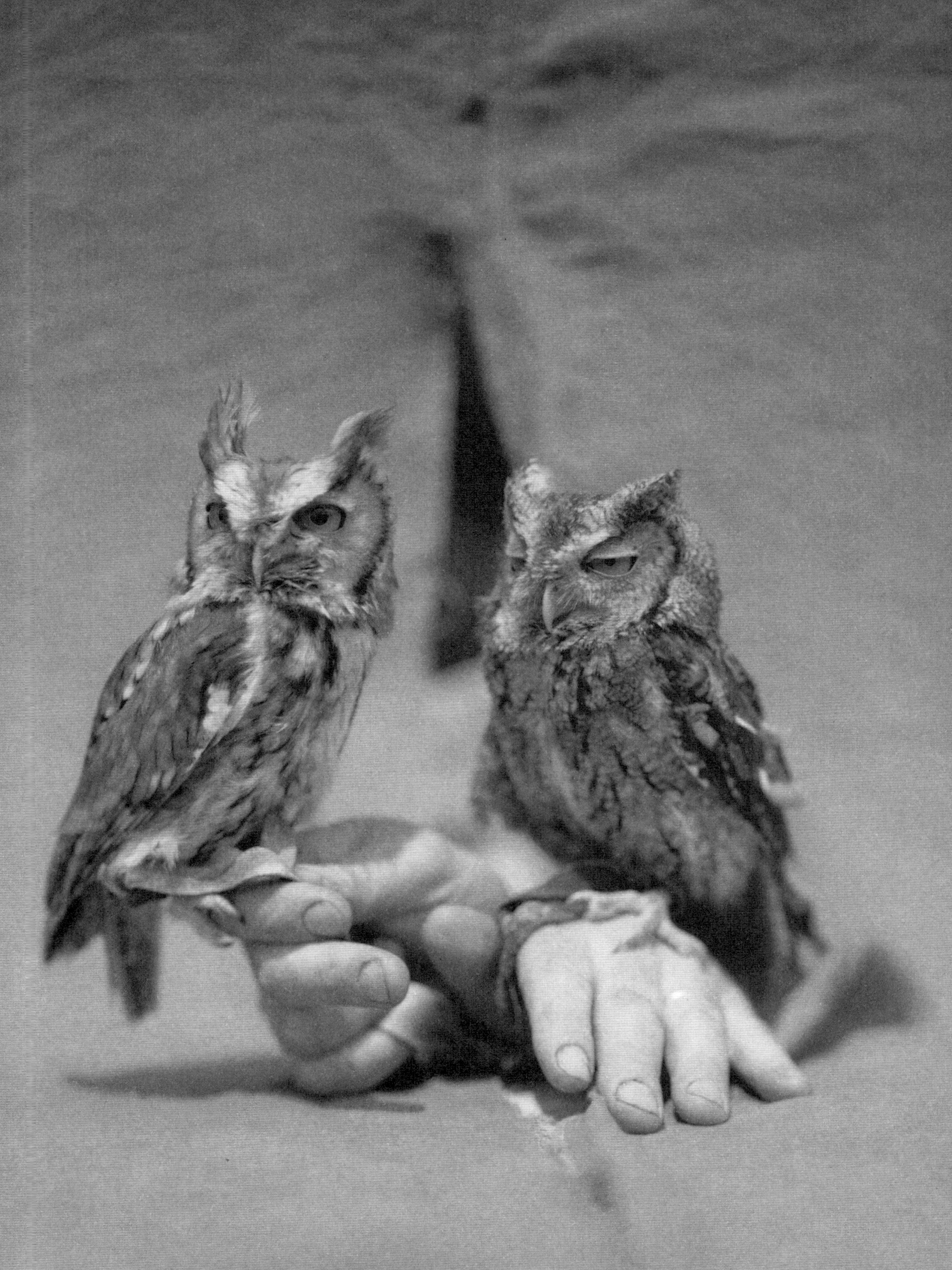

SCREECH OWLS

Mediaeval birds are closely involved with human stories and human faces. The French ethnologist, Daniel Fabre, has made a detailed study of southern European folklore and country practices to do with birds. He points out that birdnesting is an exclusively male undertaking, and the increasing difficulty of higher and more dangerous nests represents a rite of passage from childhood to manhood. The male organ has birdnames in many languages—cock in most, peru (turkey) in Portuguese, and, as Fabre points out in an enchanting article on the lonely childhood of Louis XIII of France, "guillery" (twitter [of sparrows]) was the euphemism used by the royal household checking the growth and strength of the royal appendage. It is interesting that modern English refers to women as "birds" or "chicks," whilst birdwatching and birdnesting are male activities. Two wonderful recent collections of oral literature from Southern Europe, Antonin Perbosc's *Le Langage des Bêtes* and Joan Amades' *L'Origine des Bêtes,* list folktales about how the birds acquired their shapes, colours and habits, and all sorts of human renderings of birds' calls and cries. The strangest of these, in my ears, were various versions of the hen's complaint that she is barefooted—"Vaig descalca! Vaig descalca! Vaig descalca!" which is a Catalan version of the cry of Sally Hennypenny which I learned in my childhood from Beatrix Potter's Mrs. Tiggywinkle— "I go barefoot, barefoot, barefoot!" The birdlore in *The Origin of the Beasts* follows a strange pattern—the birds are good or evil according to whether they succoured or injured Christ and the Virgin in their lives. Thus the harsh cry of the jay, according to various transcriptions, is an attempt to tell the pursuing soldiers where Mary and her child were hidden on the Flight into Egypt, or to tempt Judas to sell his master, or to tell the soldiers where Jesus was hidden. The robin has a red breast because he attempted to staunch the blood of Jesus on the Cross, whilst the magpie is an accursed bird, "the spy of the demon in the world of the birds" who has seven feathers from the devil and perched on the Cross saying, "Rac, rac, rac." The nightingale, on the other hand, sang all through the crucifixion to alleviate the pain of Jesus. The whole span of known birds is assimilated into moral and religious tales of this kind, humanised, sanctified, demonised.

There are many legends of humans who learned the language of the birds, from Siegfried hearing the thrush when he has drunk the dragon's blood, to a tale with many variations of a young man who rescued the King of Snakes from a bush, received the gift of the language of birds and beasts, married a shrew who tempted him to betray his secret and lose his life, and was saved by overhearing a cock, who explained that he had many wives, whom he beat when they asked awkward questions.

Once, on a dark night, I was dining in the House of Commons with the writer Robert Irwin, who is an expert on Arab and Persian languages and culture, and we saw what appeared to be white flashes wheeling in the sky outside a Gothic window. We went out onto the terrace overlooking the Thames and were surrounded by a myriad whirling white birds—a kind of small seagull, roosting on every available ledge, chair, and table, flying up in white hosts and settling again. "The Parliament of Fowls," said Robert, appropriately. The allegorical legend of the gathering of a parliament of birds (the word parliament deriving from the French and English for speech, discussion, language) is ancient, and Oriental in origin. Farad ud-Din Attar, the twelfth-century Persian mystic poet, wrote a long poem, *The Conference of the Birds*, in which the birds gather in search of their mystic ruler, the paradisal bird, the Simorgh, known only from a single feather which appeared in China. Attar's birds are led by the hoopoe, who encourages the fainthearted, tells moral and mystical tales, and finally reveals to the few who persist through the seven dangerous valleys of the Way that the Simorgh is themselves—thirty birds only have reached the end, and in Persian Si is thirty, and Morgh is birds. These birds are primarily images for human souls, despite some early brilliant descriptions of the Peacock, made from angels' feathers, the beast who made friends with the Snake and let him into Eden, so that his feet became hideous, the Partridge "with his Foot and Bill/Crimson with raking Rubies from the Hill/and clattering his spurs," the timid finch, and the "dapper duck demure" a self-declared sanctified observer of rituals.

Geoffrey Chaucer's *Parliament of Fowls* is a dream vision, set in a Garden, where all the birds come on St Valentine's Day to choose their mates, and various eagles dispute for the hand of the "formel eagle," the royal bird. The poem has been thought to be a political allegory about the suit of Richard II for the hand of Anne of Bohemia, and the birds are arranged in classes—eagles, worm-fowls, water-birds—representing perhaps the classes of mediaeval society. Chaucer's list is full of energy, and his birds have characters and characteristics, often done with one word.

There myghten men the royal egle fynde,
That with his sharpe lok perseth the sonne,
And othere egles of a lowere kynde,
Of whiche that clerkes wel devyse conne.
Ther was the tiraunt with his fetheres donne
And grey, I mene the goshauk, that doth pyne
To bryddes for his outrageous ravyne.

The gentyl faucoun, that with his feet distrayneth
The kynges hand; the hardy sperhauk eke,
The quayles foo; the merlioun that payneth
Hymself ful ofte the larke for to seke;
There was the douve with hire yën meke;
The jelous swan, ayens his deth that syngeth;
The oule ek, that of deth the bode bryngeth;

The crane, the geaunt, with his trompes soun;
The thef, the chough; and ek the janglynge pye;
The skornynge jay; the eles fo, heroun;
The false lapwynge, ful of trecherye;
The stare, that the conseyl can bewrye;
The tame ruddok, and the coward kyte;
The kok, that orloge is of thorpes lyte;

The sparwe, Venus sone; the nyghtyngale,
That clepeth forth the grene leves newe;
The swalwe, mortherere of the foules smale
That maken hony of floures freshe of hewe;
The wedded turtil, with hire herte trewe;
The pekok, with his aungel fetheres bryghte;
The fesaunt, scorner of the cok by nyghte;

The waker goos; the cukkow ever unkynde;
The popynjay, ful of delicasye;
The drake, stroyere of his owene kynde;
The storke, the wrekere of avouterye;
The hote cormeraunt of glotenye;
The raven wys; the crowe with vois of care;
The throstil old; the frosty feldefare.

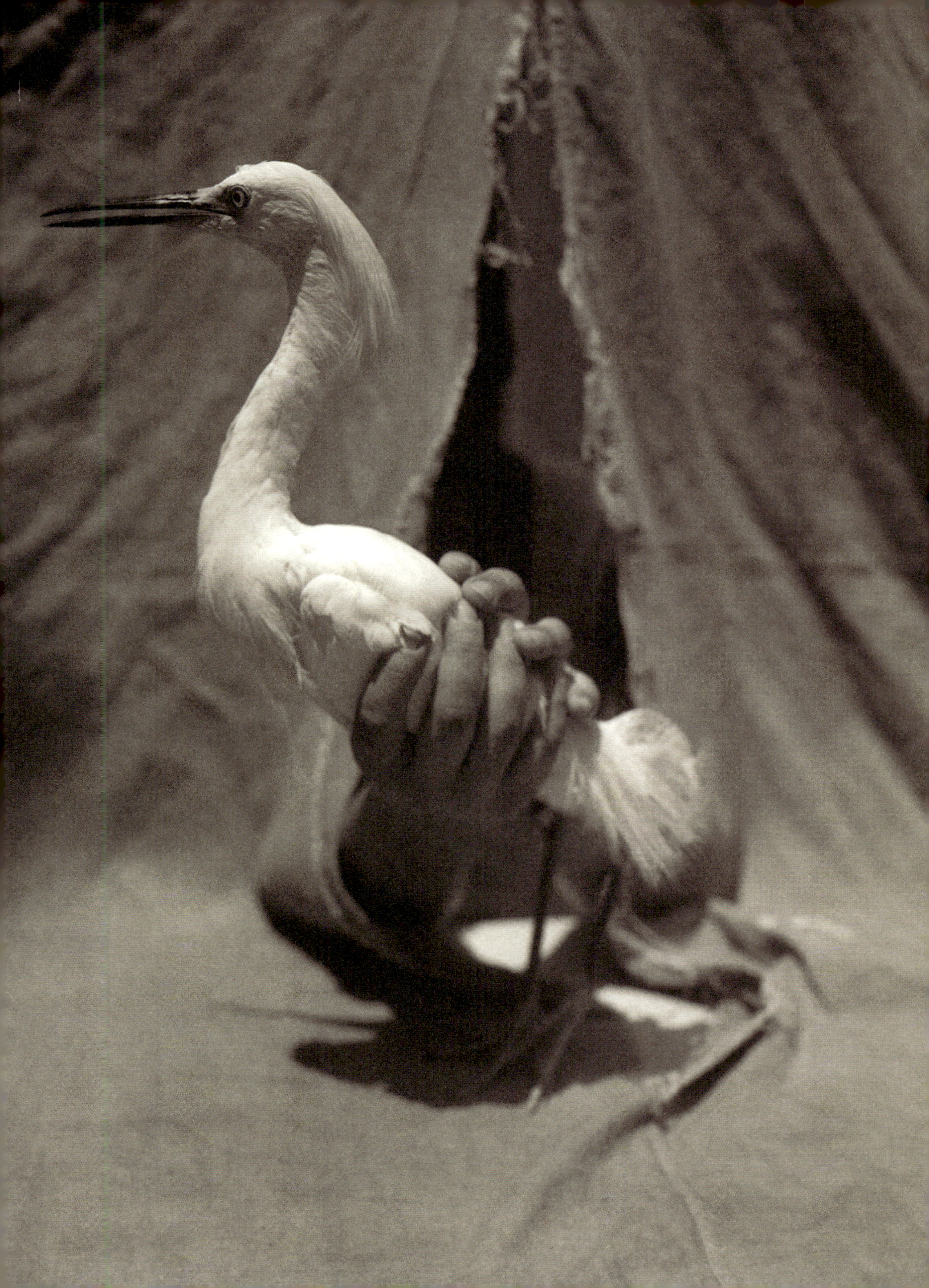

These are both social and emblematic birds; the parliament resembles a human one, the birds are diverse society with different qualities—but, like those of the bestiary and the Persian Conference of Birds, they are also emblematic of human qualities. Christian saints have had gentle relations with the creatures, particularly birds: St Malo watched over his cowl where a wren had laid an egg; Irish saints such as St Kevin are depicted with a cloud of birds resting on their outstretched arms; St Francis preached a sermon to his "sisters the birds," and stilled a wheeling flock of screaming swallows who interrupted a sermon. Saints were kind to real birds, in legendary tales; they were emblems of gentleness between man and the created world; St Brigid "blessed a frightened bird until she played with it in her hand;" the desert saints were fed by eagles. The realistic sermon to the flock of welcoming birds has an iconographic link to visionary paradisal sermons to "the spirits, the souls of the righteous, in the form of bright white birds." St Francis had a monitory dream which caused him to relinquish the leadership of his Order. "For he beheld as it were a little hen that was black and had feathered legs with feet like a tame dove, and she had so many chicks that she was not able to gather them under her own wings, but they went about in a circle round the hen, beyond her wings." The saint interprets the dream: — "I am that hen, small of stature, and by nature black, that ought to be simple as a dove, and on winged affection of the virtues to fly toward heaven. And unto me the Church hath given and will give many sons, whom I shall not be able in my own strength to protect. Whence behoveth me to commend them unto Holy Church, the which under the shadow of her wings shall protect and govern them."

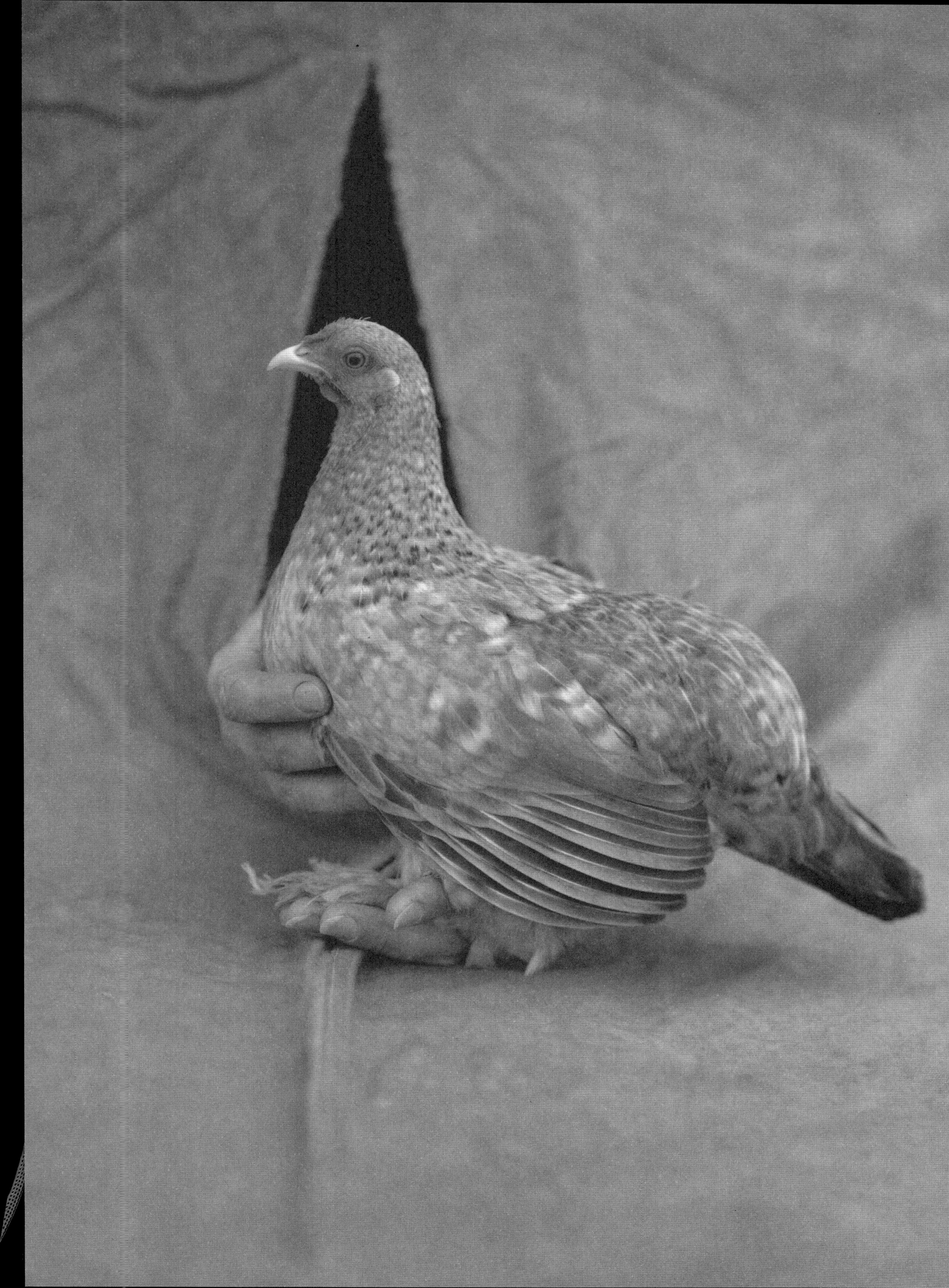

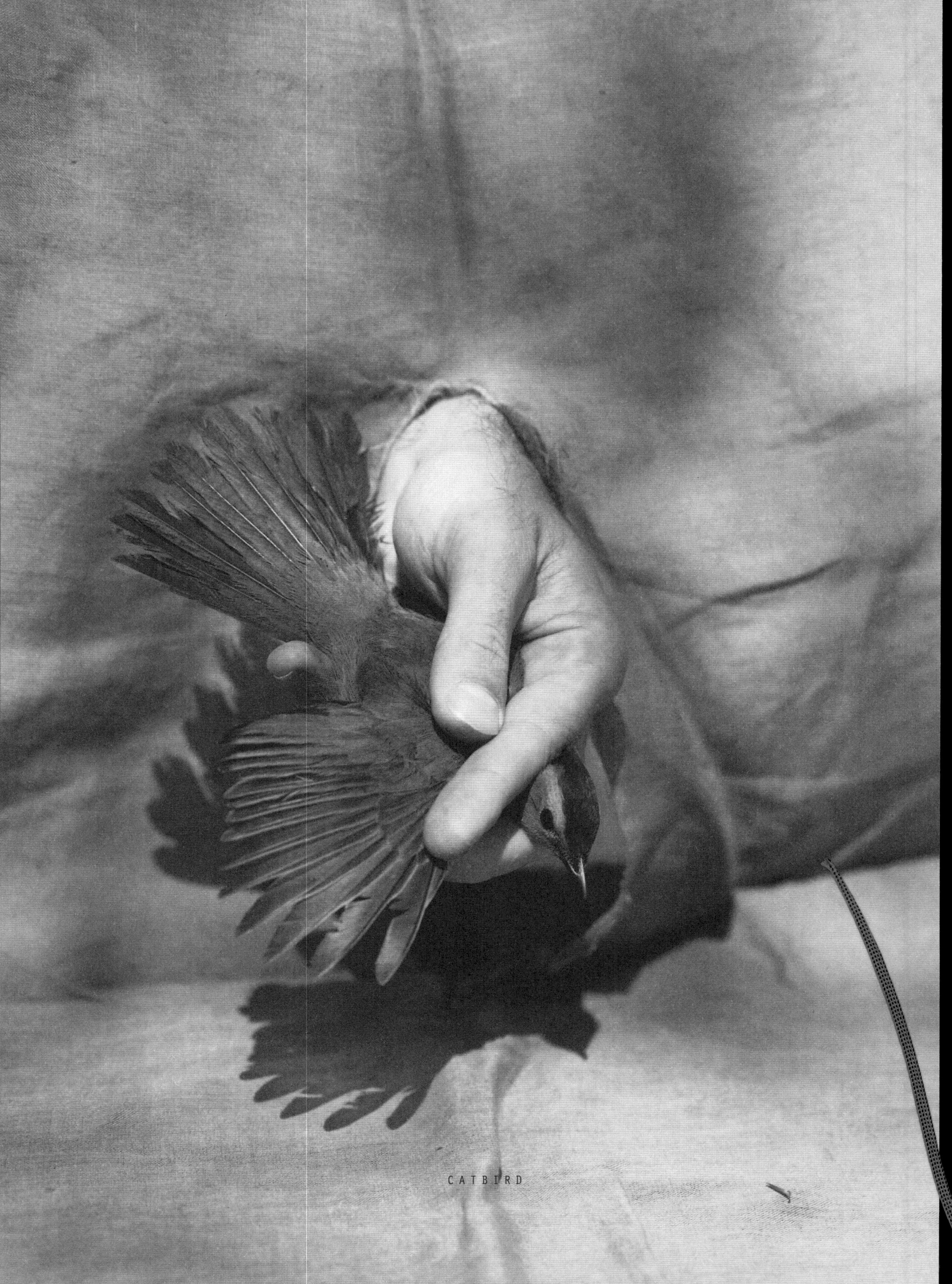

CATBIRD

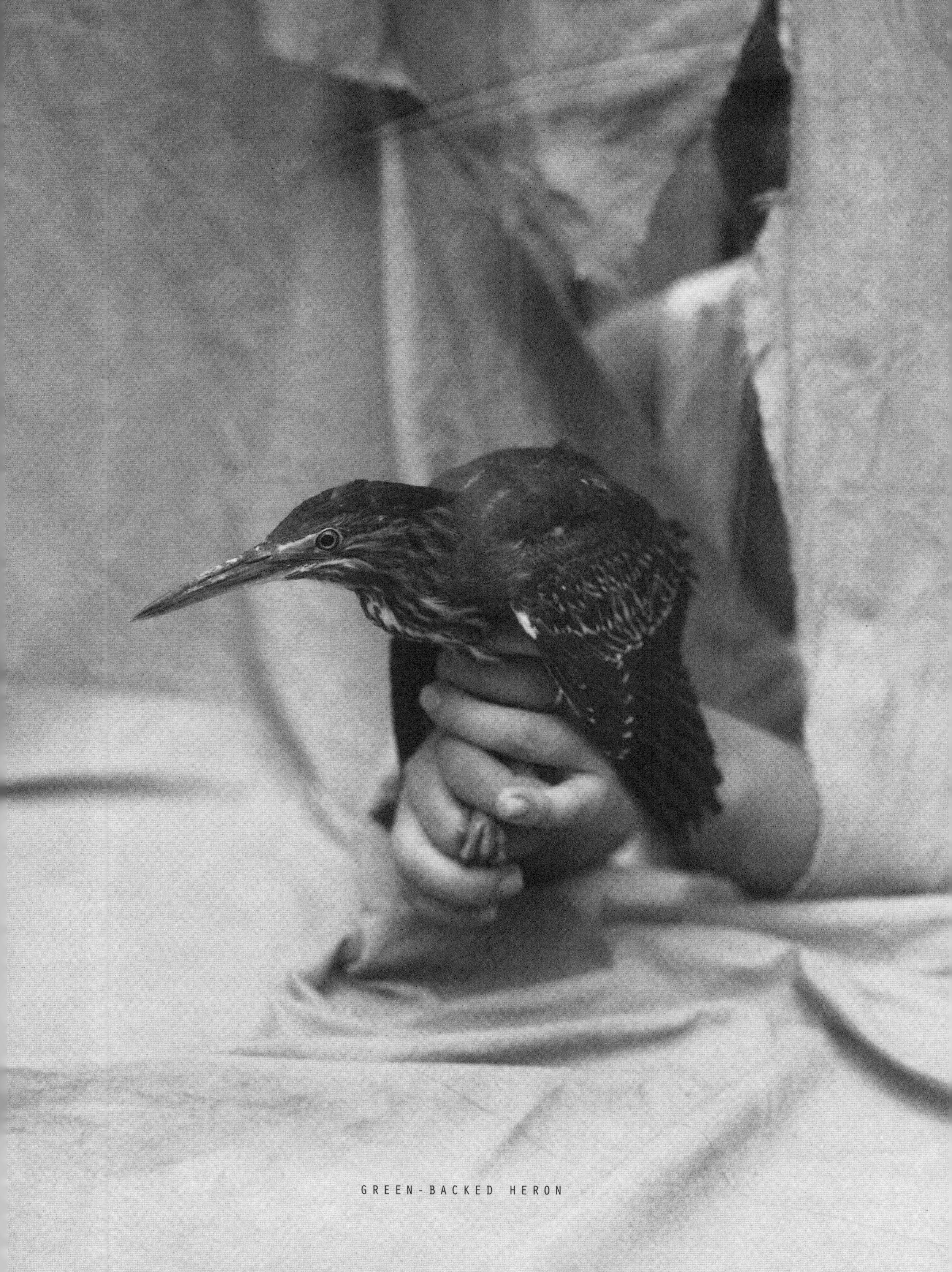

GREEN-BACKED HERON

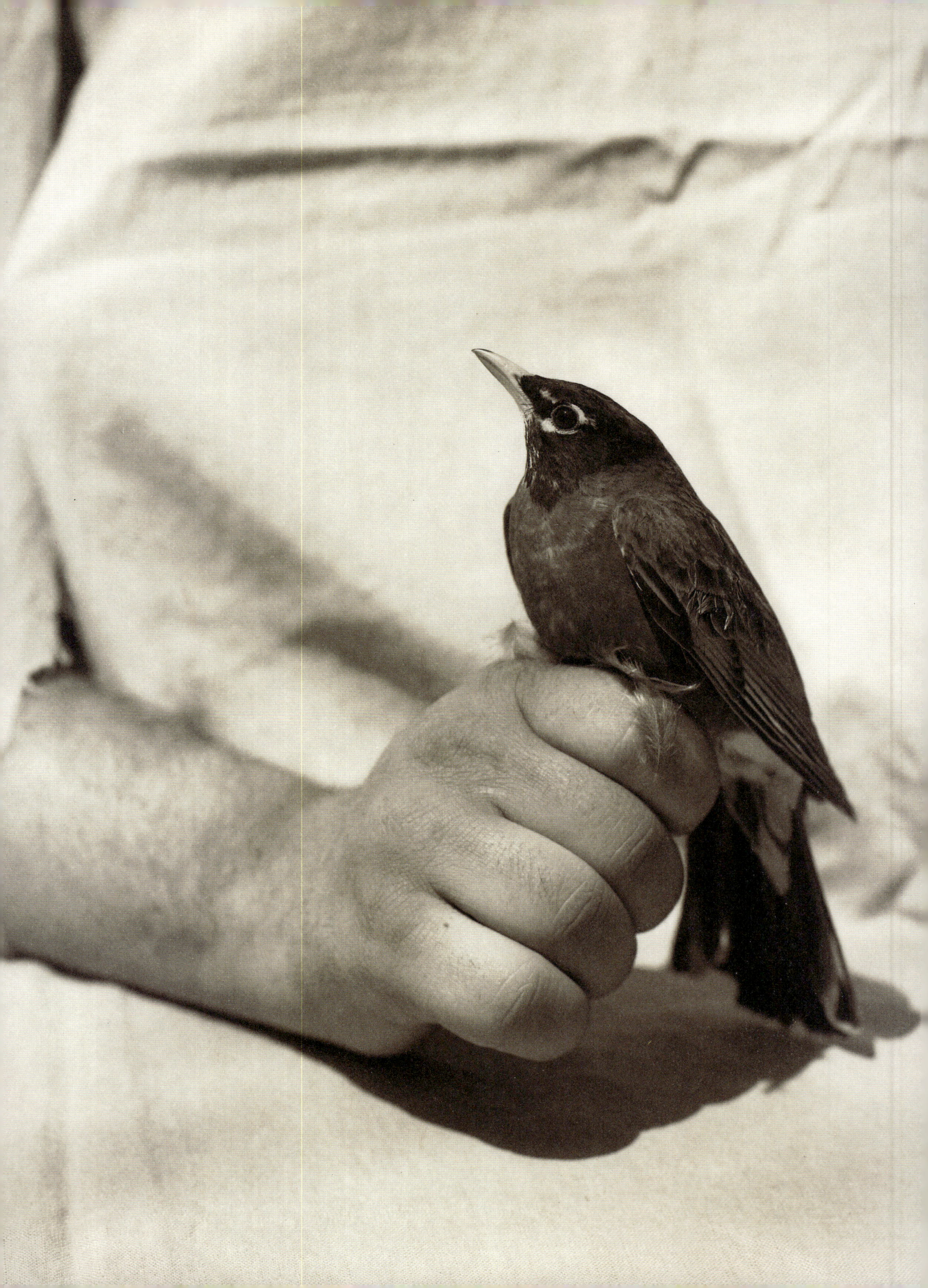

My own childhood was enriched and puzzled by the nursery rhyme of the *Death of Cock Robin*, which I vaguely felt, and feel, to be about something more important than the happenstance characteristics of the birds, assigned by the strong rhymes. Frazer, in *The Golden Bough*, has long passages about the ritual killing of the "wren king" at the winter solstice, and perhaps Cock Robin is part of all that—though part of the charm of the list of characters is the opportunist rhyming of the doggerel.

"Who killed Cock Robin?"
"I" said the sparrow,
"With my bow and arrow,
I killed Cock Robin."
"Who saw him die?"
"I" said the fly,
"With my little eye,
I saw him die."
"Who caught his blood?"
"I" said the fish,
"With my little dish.
I caught his blood."
"Who'll make his shroud?"
"I" said the beetle,
"With my thread and needle
I'll make his shroud."
"Who'll bear the torch?"
"I" said the linnet,
"Will come in a minute.
I'll bear the torch."
"Who'll be the clerk?"
"I" said the lark,
"I'll say Amen in the dark.
I'll be the clerk."
"Who'll dig his grave?"
"I" said the owl,
"With my spade and my trowel
I'll dig his grave."
"Who'll be the parson?"
"I" said the rook,
"With my little book
I'll be the parson."
"Who'll be the chief mourner?"
"I" said the dove,
"I mourn for my love.
I'll be chief mourner."
"Who'll sing his dirge?"
"I" said the thrush,
"As I sing in the bush.
I'll sing his dirge."
"Who'll carry his coffin?"
"I" said the kite,
"If it be in the night.
"I'll carry the coffin."
"Who'll toll the bell?"
"I" said the bull,
"Because I can pull
I'll toll the bell."
All the birds in the air
Fell sighing and sobbing
When they heard the bell toll
For poor Cock Robin.

I used to love to recite this as a child, and think now that it gave me a complex pleasure with its interweaving of two lists—the list of the last rites and the list of creatures, predominantly birds, the death made orderly by chanting, the whole of nature implicated in the death of a robin. I always associated it with the song Bottom tries to sing in *A Midsummer Night's Dream*, to keep his spirits up when he has been transfigured into an ass, an English list of comfortable English birds, whistling and chirping...

"The ousel cock, so black of hue
With orange-tawny bill
The throstle, with his note so true,
The wren with little quill—
The finch, the sparrow and the lark
The plain-song cuckoo gray,
Whose note full many a man doth mark
And dares not answer nay."

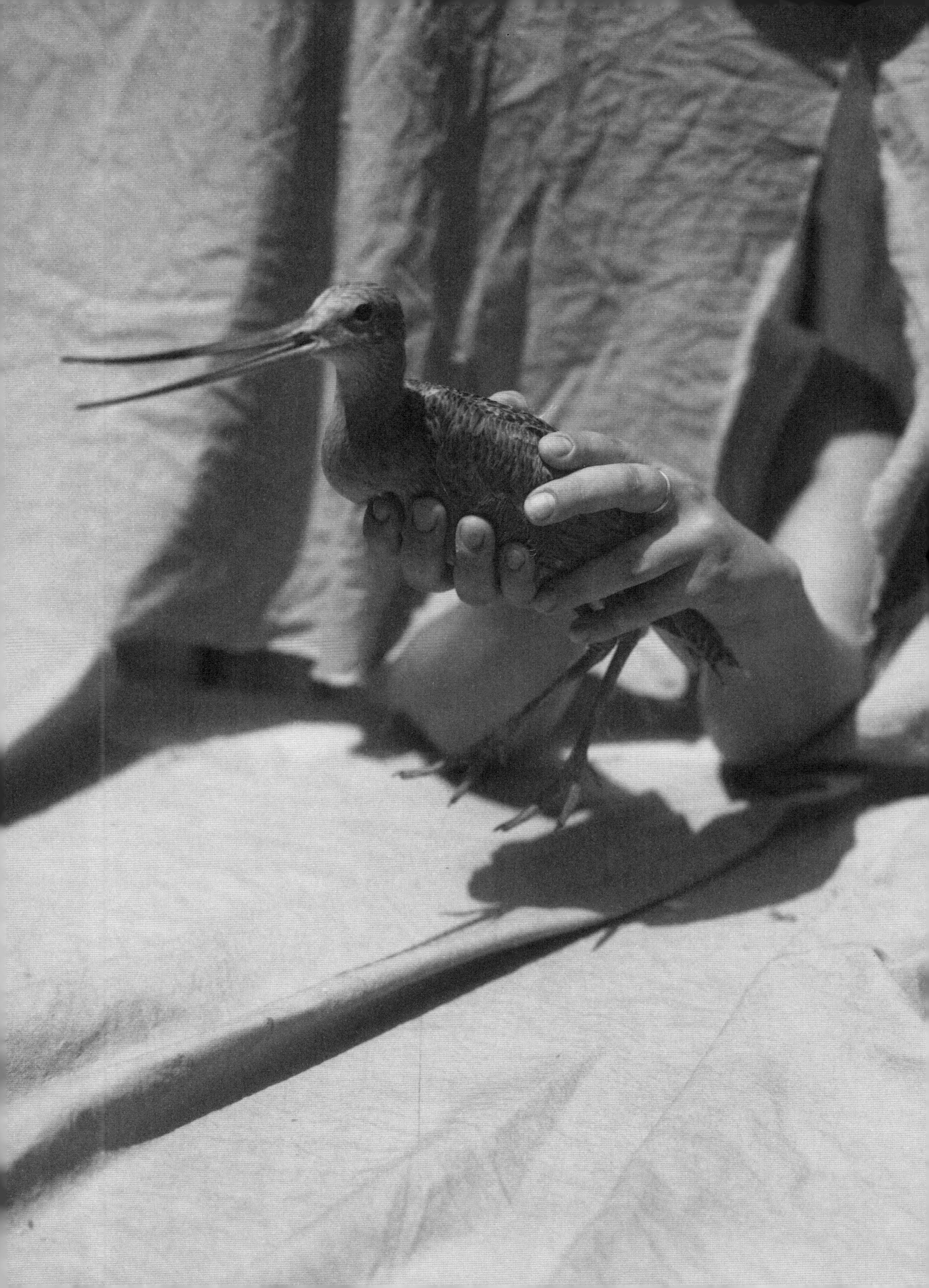

Most of the lists I have quoted so far have been about a kind of border between human and avian qualities; lists which read and assimilate birds into human life and thought. Here is a list from the mediaeval Boke of St Albans by Dame Juliana Berners—a formal list of the names of groups of birds, where the metaphors are to a modern ear unexpected and poetic.

THE COMPANYES OF BESTYS AND FOULES

An Herde of swannys
An Herde of cranys
An Herde of corlewys
An Herde of wrennys
A Nye of fesauntys
A Bevy of quayles
A Sege of herons
A Sege of bytourys
A Sorde or a Sute of malards
A Mustre of pecockys
A Walke of snytes
An Exaltynge of larkys
A Cherme of goldfynches
A Flyghte of Doves
An Unkyndnes of Ravens
A Claterynge of choughes
A Dyssymulacioun of byrdes
A Bevy of conyes
A Cowple of spanellys
A Tryppe of Harys
A Gagle of geys
A Brode of hennys
A Badelynge of dokys
A Covy of pertryche
A Sprynge of telys
A Desserte of lapwynges
A Falle of wodcockes
A Congregacion of plovers
A Coverte of cootes
A Duell of turtylles
A Tygendis of pyes
A Flyght of swalowes
A Buyldynge of rokys
A Murmuracion of stares
A Nest of rabettys.

The modern British sportsman's terms for wildfowl hunted has also its poetry, but lacks the anthropomorphic emotions, like the Unkindness of Ravens, or the Dissimulation of birds.

A herd of swans
A gaggle of geese (when on the water)
A skein of geese (when on wing)
A paddling of ducks (when on water)
A team of wild-ducks (when flying in the air)
A sord or suit of mallards
A company of widgeon
A flight or rush of dunbirds
A spring of teal
A dropping of sheldrakes
A covert of coots
A herd of curlews
A sedge of herons
A wing or congregation of plovers
A desert of lapwings
A walk of snipes
A fling of oxbirds
A hill of ruffs
A small number of wildfowl, as ducks and geese (about thirty or forty) is termed a "trip." The same of widgeon, dunbirds or teal, is termed a "bunch"; and a smaller number, from ten to twenty, is called a "little knob."

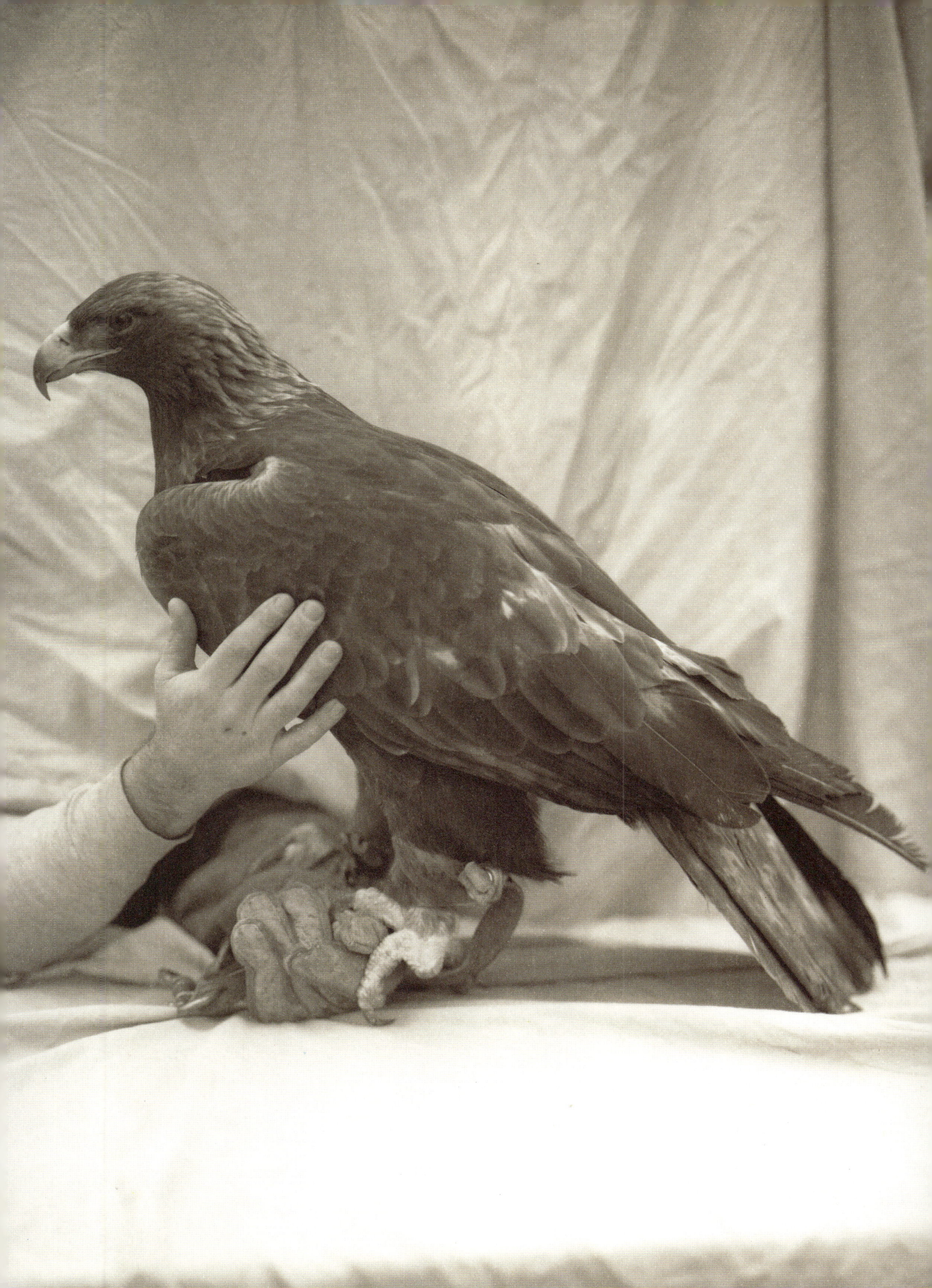

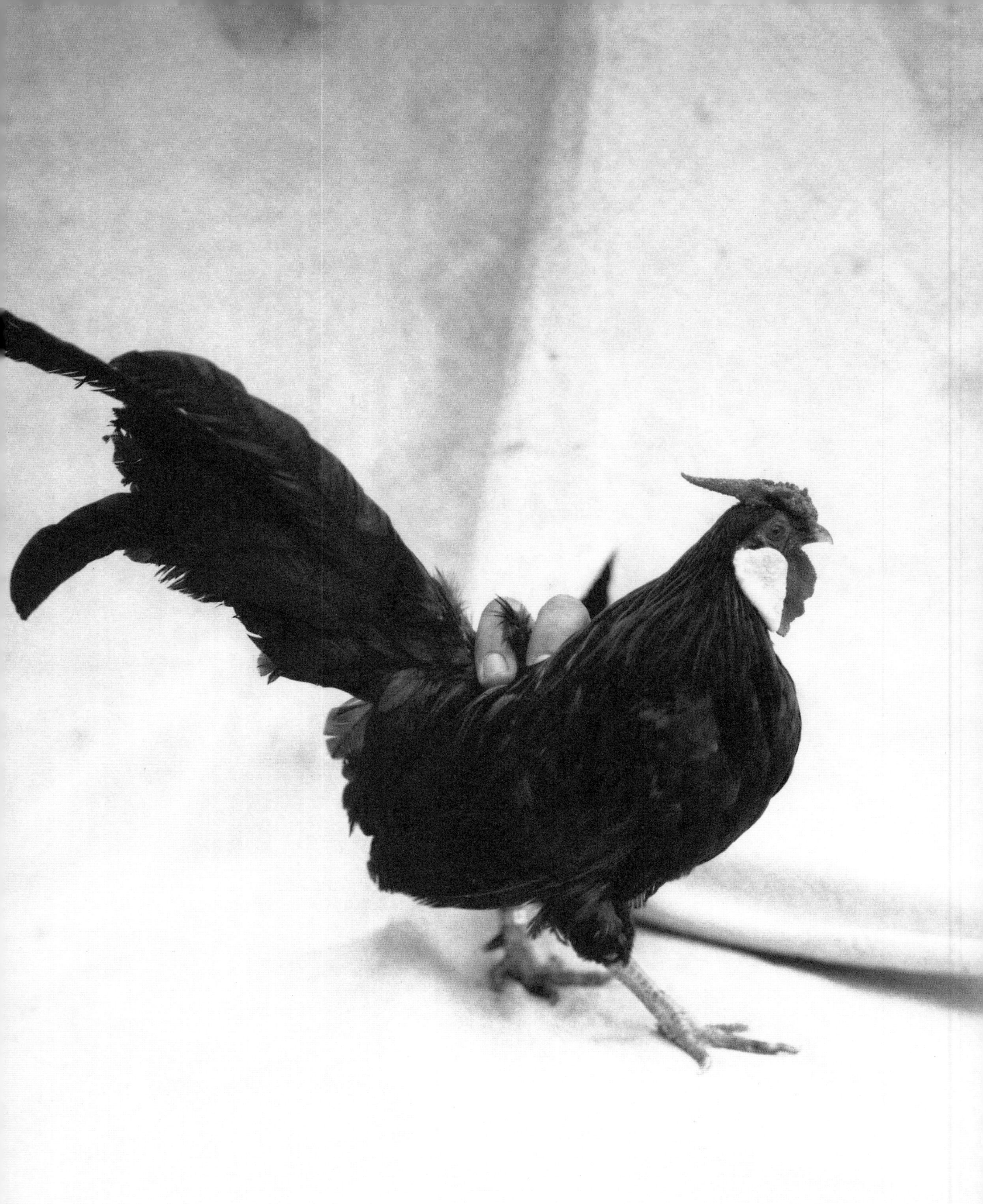

BLACK ROSECOMB CHICKEN

Perhaps the most diligent scientific namer of birds was Carl Linnaeus, who in eighteenth century Sweden constructed his *Systema Naturae*, defining species and genera. There is a modern impatience with Linnaeus' classifying and dissecting mind, which in my view quite misses the extraordinary poetry both of his passionate interest in the natural world, and of his choice of names for plants and insects—he named species and genera of tropical butterflies for the Greek and Trojan warriors of Homer, for the gods and nymphs of classical mythology—a form of colonisation, or humanisation, which left the creatures what they were, but produced endless lovely metaphors for the contemplative mind. Linnaeus' *Methodus Avium*, written in the 1720's, was the first classification of birds according to the method of distinguishing between genera and species that is still used—he worked by observing and classifying differences in beak and claw, and his biographer Knut Hagberg observes, "one wonders if there were not also a purely aesthetic feeling behind this concept, a sense of form in keeping with that of the painter and the sculptor.... In *Methodus Avium* he has seen—seen quite sensuously with his bright eyes, seen the birds as Leonardo saw the human muscles—that birds of prey, parrots, owls, all the

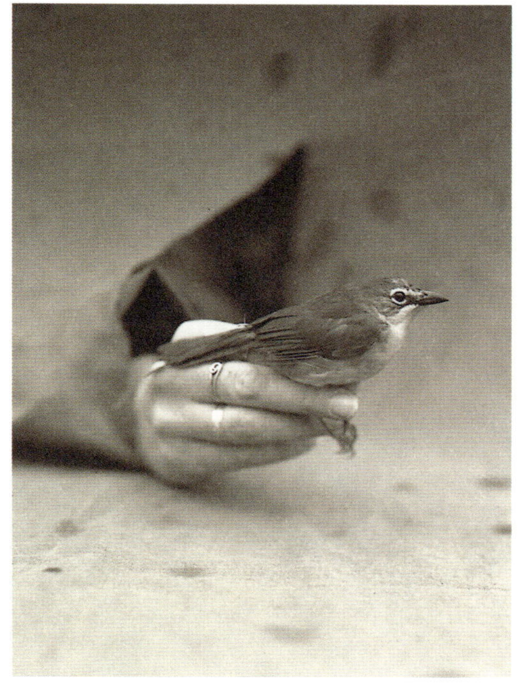

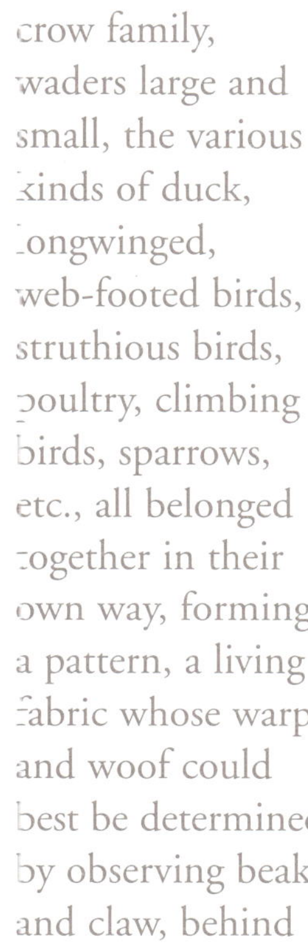

crow family, waders large and small, the various kinds of duck, longwinged, web-footed birds, struthious birds, poultry, climbing birds, sparrows, etc., all belonged together in their own way, forming a pattern, a living fabric whose warp and woof could best be determined by observing beak and claw, behind the empiric method is an aesthetic conception." Linnaeus attended the lectures of Olof Rudbeck the younger, who illustrated his talks with detailed coloured drawings of birds, but mixed scientific curiosity with a deference to ancient authority and Biblical classifications. Some notes have survived from 1727–8 in which he discusses systems of classification:

"I find, concerning the method, that Gesnerus, who has followed the alphabet, has little or no system. Aldrovandus, on the other hand, begins with the largest birds, the eagle, the kite, the long-eared owl and so on, but as *natura non fecit saltum*, I humbly maintain that it is better to begin with the delicate and smaller ones and so work up to the others.... Yet we also find in the Holy Scriptures that the birds have been classified; for in Gen. I is mentioned *ops calaps*, which is the same as *avis calata*, and may mean the water birds, those we call *palmipedes* or swimming birds, which the Jews were forbidden to eat because of their train-oil taste, just as noxious and unclean animals were forbidden because of leprosy. More particularly in Lev. XI v.13 there are to be found the following words

"And these are they which ye shall have in an abomination among the fowls; they shall not be eaten, they are an abomination: the eagle and ossifrage and the ospray, And the vulture, and the kite after his kind; Every raven after his kind; And the owl, and the night hawk, and the cuckow and the hawk after his kind, And the little owl, and the cormorant, and the great owl, And the swan, and the pelican, and the gier eagle, And the stork, the heron after her kind, and lapwing, and the bat, All fowls that creep, going upon all four shall be an abomination to you."

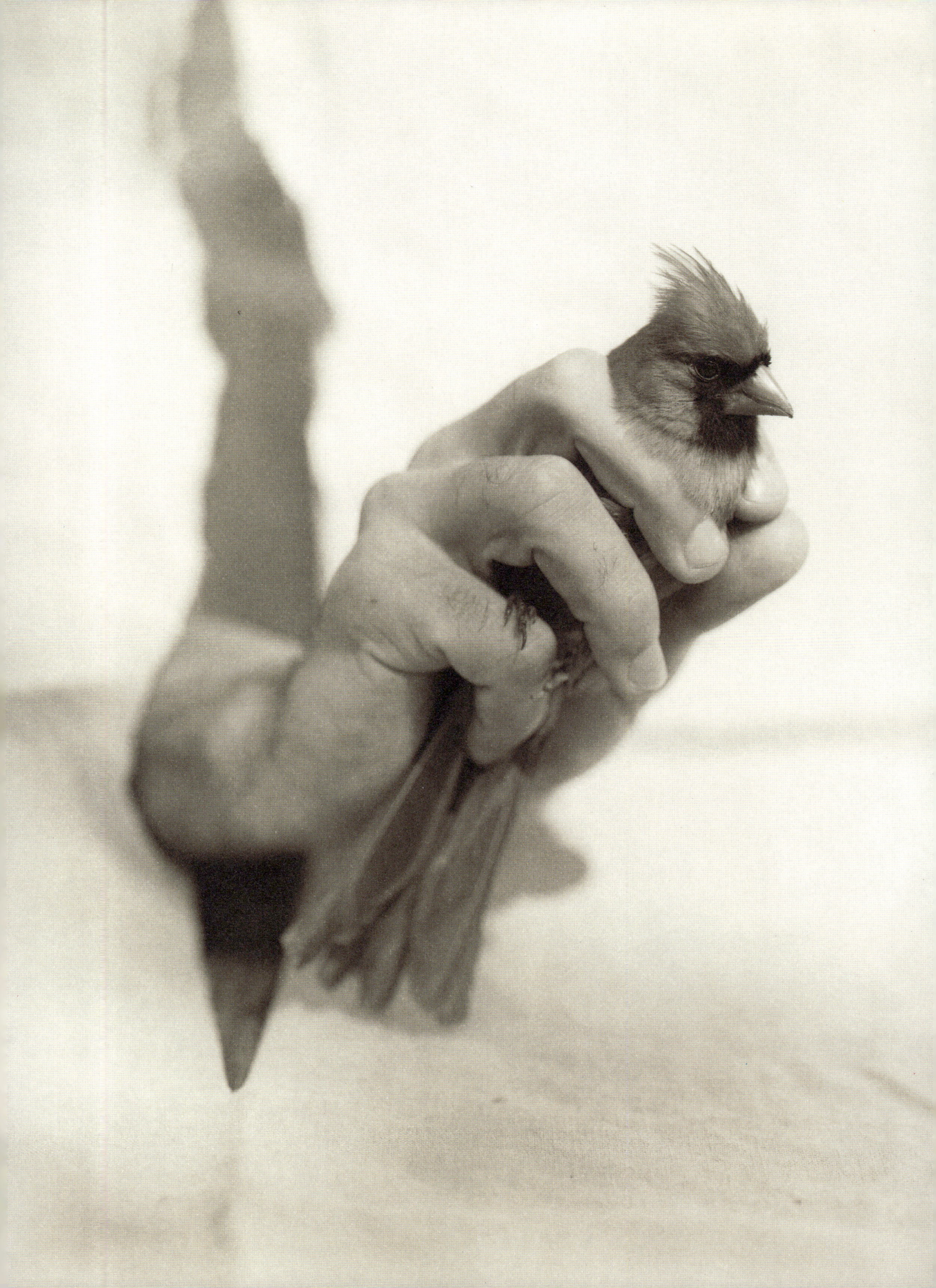

Knut Hagberg comments that the theologians among Rudbeck's audience were interested in the religious and philological comments; the future scientists were interested in the accuracy of the lifesize illustrations, "resolving thereafter to isolate concrete observations of nature from theological and philosophical speculations. Through this decision the snake of the age changed its skin." Linnaeus himself accepted many beliefs on authority, including Aristotle's statement that swallows wintered under ice in lakes and ponds, but his classification of the birds in his *Systema Naturae* is a quite different list from the bestiaries.

AVES (Birds)

i. Accipiters: including vultures, falcons, hawks, kites, eagles, buzzards, owls, shrikes.

ii. Picae: including parrots, toucans, crows, rollers, birds-of-paradise, cuckoos, kingfishers, bee-eaters, tree-creepers etc.

iii. Anseres: including ducks, swans, geese, auks, petrels, pelicans, albatross, tropic-bird, divers, grebes, gulls, terns, etc.

iv. Grallae: including flamingo spoonbill, herons, cranes, snipe woodcock, avocet, coots, rails, bustards, ostrich, etc.

v. Gallinae: including gamebirds in general, peacock, pheasants, grouse.

vi. Passeres: including pigeons and doves, larks, starlings, thrushes, finches, titmice, swallows, nightjars, etc.

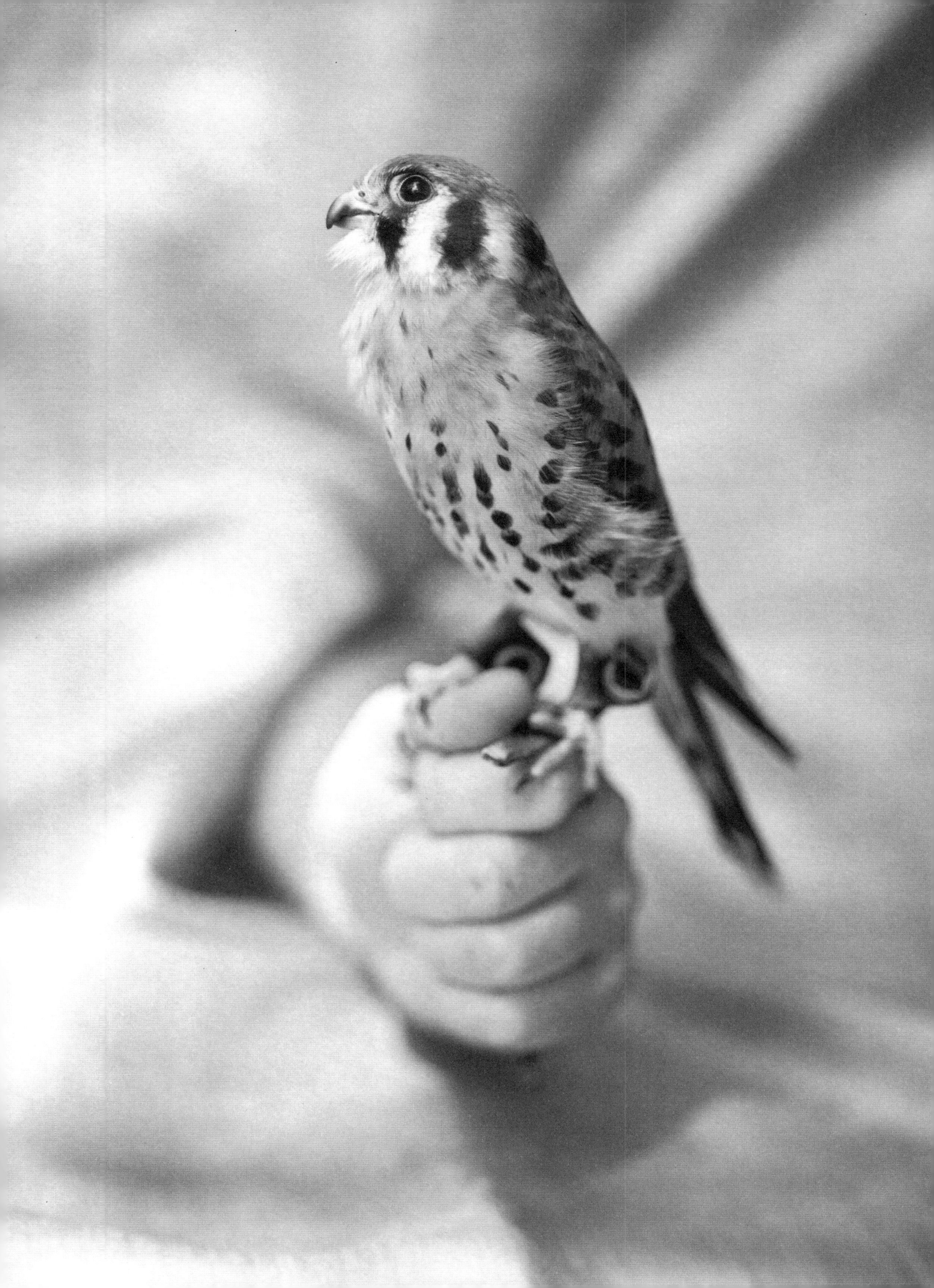

In the late eighteenth and early nineteenth centuries, travelling naturalists went all over the world, observing, classifying, collecting, naming, shooting, skinning, and mounting. The travels of Bates, Spruce, and Wallace on the Amazon are tales of immense quiet courage, pure intellectual curiosity, and a new delight in the variety and complexity of the natural world. There is a sense of abundance in the largely uninhabited worlds they enter and name. They shoot the birds they see for science and pleasure and food, as though there is no question of any lessening of the flocks. My next list is a long quotation from John James Audubon's *Mississippi River Journal* of 1820. Audubon's brilliant *Birds of America* is still startling in its beauty and novelty of vision. He also wrote a five-volume *Ornithological Biography*. His ambition was to draw and describe all the birds of America, and he named several new species—it is interesting to come across the term "nondescript" in his writings and realise that it means, not "undistinguished" but literally, *undescribed*, uncatalogued, a new species. His Mississippi journal is full of feathers and claws and gizzards, of weather and wind and water and skies, of fast-moving flocks and dipping ducks.
What follows gives an idea of his relations with his bird-world.

Sunday August 12th 1821
Arrived at the Swamp and there saw a great Number of Small Birds. Shot a beautifull *new* species of Fly Catcher Muscicapa, which I will give you Tomorow when my Drawing of it Will be finished. I had the pleasure of seing Two that appeared Much alike, they were quarelling when I shot at them but fell only One—cannot say any More of this truly handsome bird having never seen any thing of them before to Day—

Saw within a few fet a beautiful *Mourning Warbler* but Was so situated Knee deep in the Mud that I could Not retrograde without alarming it I preferred gazing at it as it innocently gazed at Me hoping it would fly at a Short distance but it Moved with a *Tweet* and out of sight in an instant. Much disapointed at My having lost the only oppr[y] I Ever have had of procuring this rare bird.

Shot several of the *Yellow Throated Warbler* all alike and all Males the woods were full of them and yet Not a femelle could I Shot—they Move sideways on the small limbs of the Cypress in a Hoping Manner extremely quickly hang often to the ends of Limbs like the titmouse and run up and down the Large Trunks much like the Nuthatches

—Killed Many *Blue Yellow back Warblers.* Saw many *Prothonotarys,* several *Watter Thrushes* that I consider More Like Warblers the Habits of Which genus they exhibit to a very great degree and the Bill of Which they have—Alligators as numerous as before basking in the Sun that this *dat was more than ordinarily uncomfortable—saw several Ibiss at respectful Distances in their common dull postures—

My Litle fly Catcher had only one wing touch[d] When I presented Myself to pick it up, it spread its tail & open its Wings and Snap its bill about 20 times in the Manner that Many of this Genus do when they seize a fly, particularly those that are Nearest the Standard of the Genus.—I seldom have seen a bird of Such Small size With so Large & beautifull an Eye. I took it home to James Perrie's Es[qr] and had the pleasure of drawing it While a live and full of Spirit, it often Made off from My fingers by starting Suddenly and unexpectedly, and then would hop round the room as quick as Carolina or Winter Wren would have done, uttering its tweet tweet tweet all the while, and Snapping every time I took it up. I put it in a Cage for a few Moments but it obstinatly forced the fore part of its head through the Lower part of the Wires and I relieved it by Confining it in My hat for the Night anxious to see More of its Movements...

Length of the *Cypress Swamp Fly Catcher Muscicapa Rara* 5 1/4 Inches—breadth 7 3/4 Inches Whole upper parts handsome ash Color appearing blue at a distance, the front of the Head mixed with Yellow, a Yellow Line Surround the Eye that is very Large Iriss deep *brown, pupil Black, between the eye & Bill & under the eye shaded with darker ash Tail Coverts lighter than the back, tail slightly forked of 12 Feathers all plain bronish ash shafts deep brown as well as those of the wings under tail Coverts Long & White—the Throat breast belly & Vent Rich citron Yellow without intermission of Shade in any of these parts. Breast spotted with black forming small chains fallin to the beginning of the spurious wings—Bill, hooked at the Tip and broad at the base. Legs feet & Claws horn Colors the last Long and Sharp Nostrils very prominent, Tongue much jagged, Mouth flesh colord & furnish outwardly With many Long black bristles—it proved a Male. Gizzard fleshy filled with wings of different Insects—Cheeks also ash col[d] My Drawing a very excellent one—finding this Bird very Weak in the Morning Killed it and put it in Whiskey—

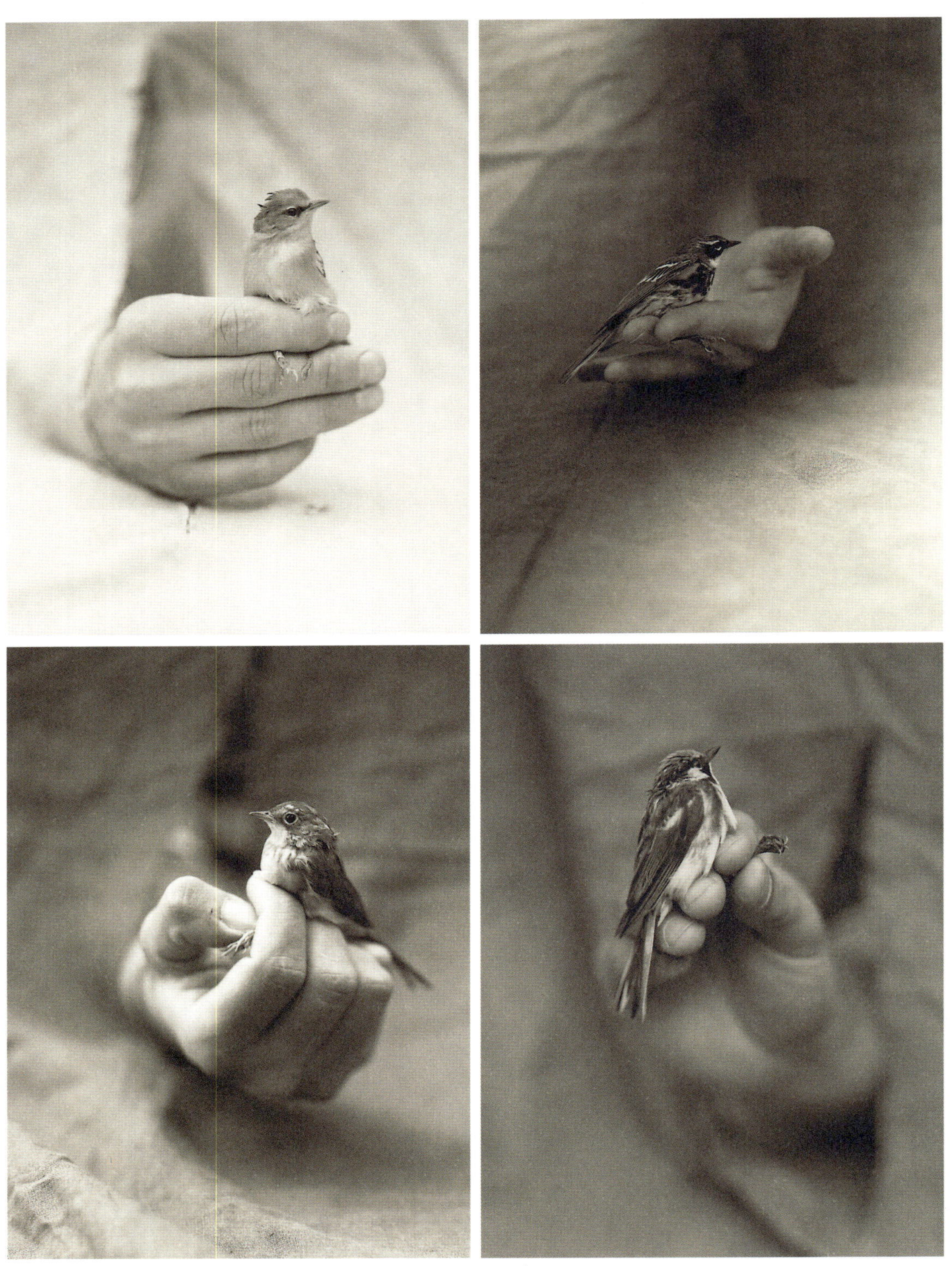

BLUE-WINGED WARBLER

MYRTLE WARBLER

CANADA WARBLER

CHESTNUT-SIDED WARBLER

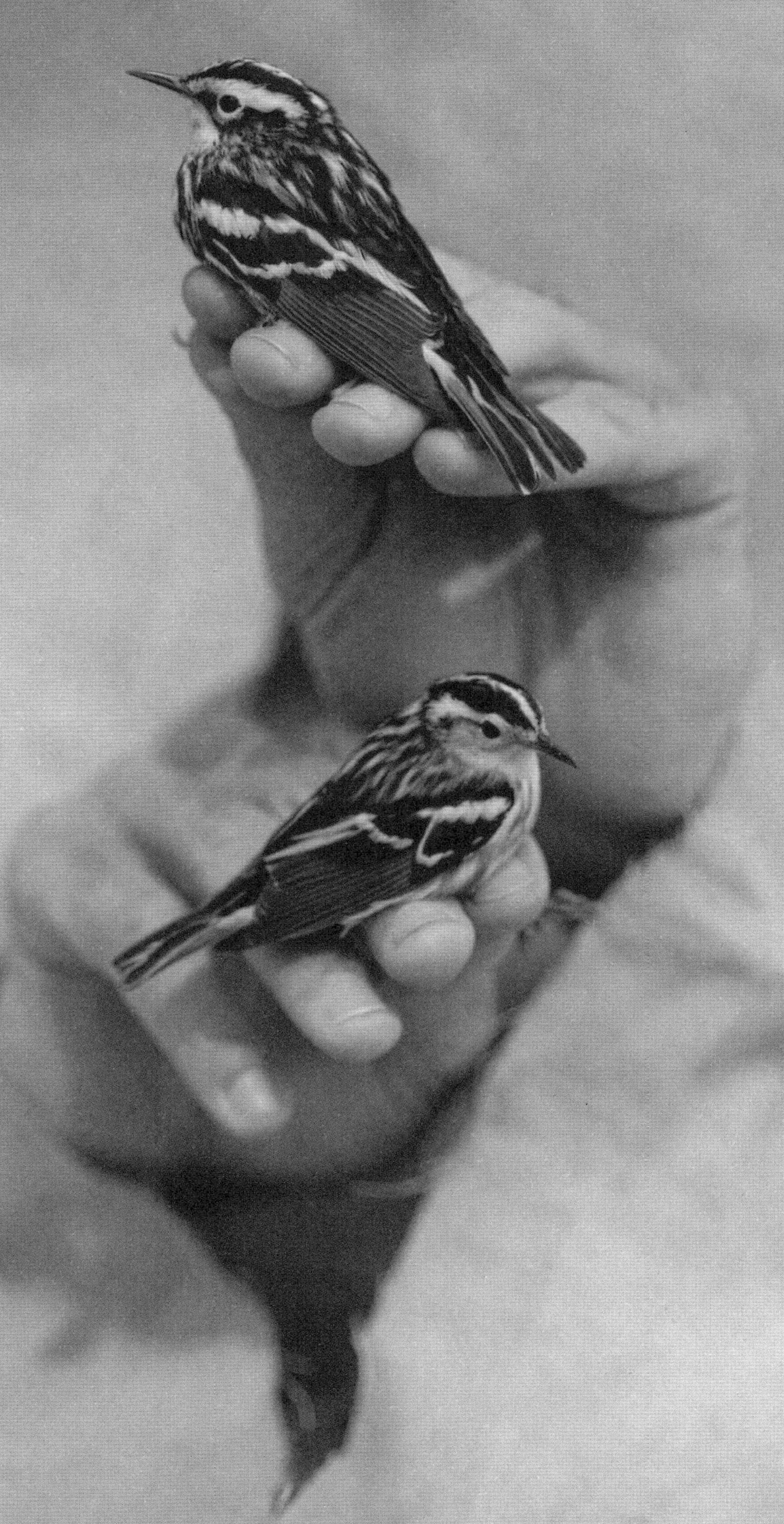

BLACK & WHITE WARBLERS

Audubon was a hunter-gatherer amongst ornithologists. Gilbert White's *The Natural History of Selborne*, published in 1789, the year of the French Revolution, is one of the classics of natural observation. White spent much time attempting to ascertain which birds migrated, and to where, asking himself a true scientist's questions about why birds such as goldfinches congregated in large flocks at certain times of the year—was there an instinct of congregation as there was one of sexual pairing in the spring? Why do birds mass in one place in bad weather, when food is scarce and might be better found by dispersing? The winter behaviour of hirundines, swallows, and house-martins was a persisting puzzle to him—he tended to believe Linnaeus. Observing the autumn congregation of swallows he writes

"But what struck me most was, that from the time they began to congregate, forsaking the chimneys and houses, they roosted every night in the osier beds of the aits of the river. Now this resorting towards that element, at that season of the year, seems to give some countenance to the northern opinion (strange as it is) of their retiring under water. A Swedish naturalist is so much persuaded of that fact, that he talks, in his calendar of *Flora* as familiarly of the swallow's going under water in the beginning of September, as he would of his poultry going to roost a little before sunset."

He returns frequently to the same question; six years later he draws the same conclusion from his careful recording of the swallows' early spring appearances.

"The house-swallow, or chimney-swallow, is undoubtedly the first comer of all the british hirundines; and appears in general on or about the thirteenth of April, as I have remarked from many years' observation. Not but now and then a straggler is seen much earlier...It is worth remarking that these birds are seen first about lakes and mill-ponds; and it is also very particular, that if these early visitors happen to find frost and snow, as was the case of the two dreadful springs of 1770 and 1771, they immediately withdraw for a time. A circumstance this much more in favour of hiding than migration; since it is much more probable that a bird should retire to its hibernaculum just at hand, than return for a week or two only to warmer latitudes."

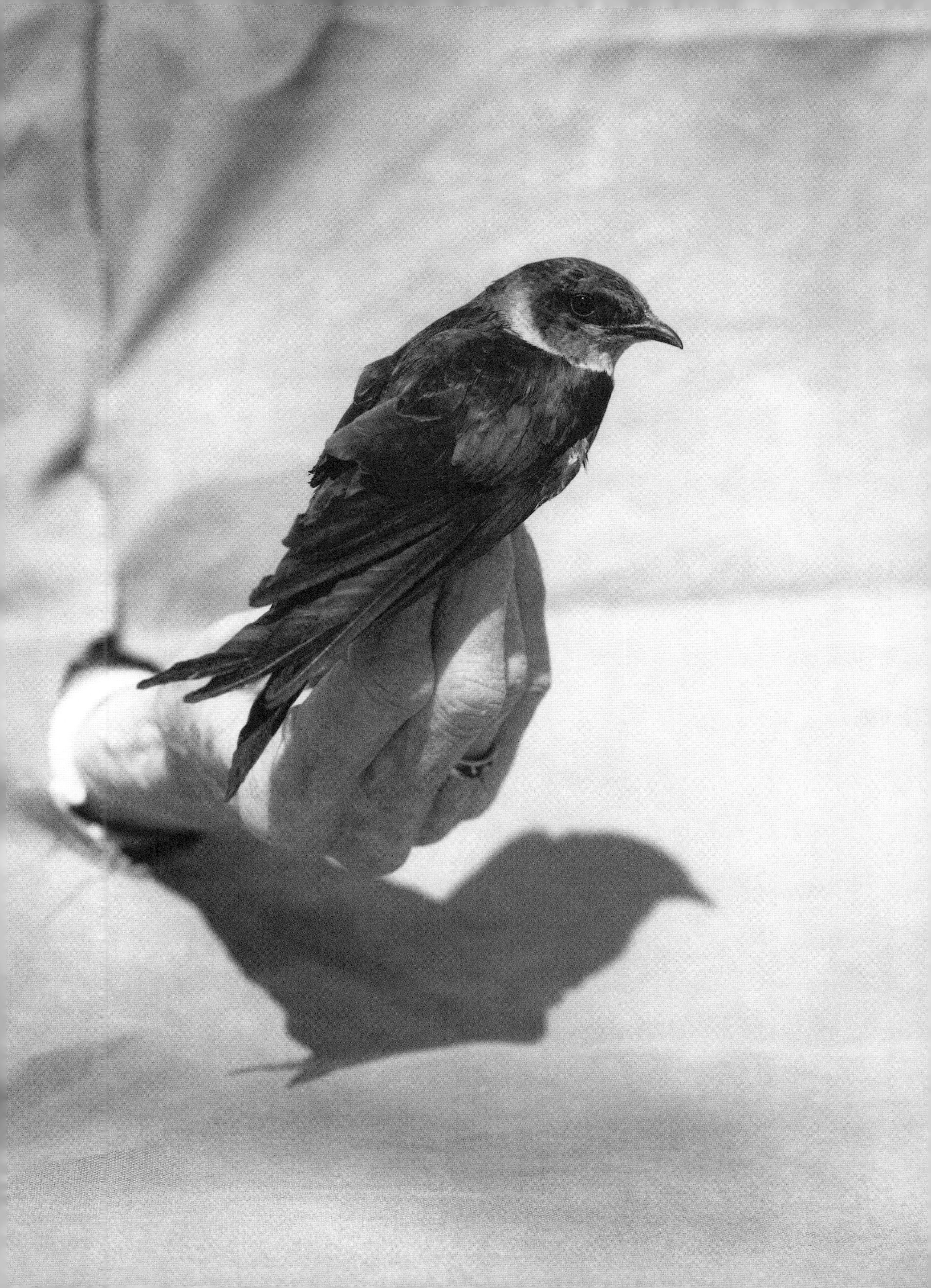

The conclusion and the reasoning are erroneous, but the precise curiosity is part of a new relation between humans and creatures. Gilbert White's prose, like Audubon's paintings, has delighted the same curiosity in subsequent generations; they are both informative and beautiful. Here is Gilbert White's masterly list of birds on the wing and their behaviour, beautifully noted and beautifully written, for the sake of the knowledge and the imaginative identification, but in no way anthropomorphic.

"Selborne August 7th 1778
A good ornithologist should be able to distinguish birds by their air as well as by their colours and shape; on the ground as well as on the wing, and in the bush as well as in the hand. For, though it must not be said that every species of bird has a manner peculiar to itself, yet there is somewhat in most *genera* at least, that at first sight discriminates them, and enables a judicious observer to pronounce on them with some certainty. Put a bird in motion

Et vera incessu patuit...

Thus kites and buzzards sail round in circles with wings expanded and motionless; and it is from their gliding manner that the former are still called in the north of England *gleads* from the Saxon verb *glidan*, to glide. The kestrel, or windhover, has a peculiar mode of hanging in the air in one place, his wings all the time being briskly agitated. Hen-harriers fly low over heaths or fields of corn, and beat the ground regularly like a pointer or setting dog. Owls move in a buoyant manner, as if lighter than air; they seem to want ballast. There is a peculiarity belonging to ravens that must draw the attention even of the most incurious—they spend all their leisure time in striking and cuffing each other on the wing in a kind of playful skirmish; and when they move from one place to another, frequently turn on their backs with a loud croak, and seem to be falling to the ground. When this odd gesture betides them, they are scratching themselves with one foot, and then lose the centre of gravity. Rooks sometimes dive and tumble in a frolicksome manner; crows and daws swagger in their walk; woodpeckers fly *volatu undoso* opening and closing their wings at every stroke, and so are always rising or falling in curves. All of this genus use their tails, which incline downward, as a support while they run up trees. Parrots, like all other hook-clawed birds, walk aukwardly, and make use of their bill as a third foot, climbing and descending with ridiculous caution. All the *gallinae* parade and walk gracefully, and run nimbly; but fly with difficulty, with an impetuous whirring, and in a straight line. Magpies and jays flutter with powerless wings, and make no dispatch; herons seem encumbered with too much sail for their light bodies; but these vast hollow wings are necessary in carrying burdens, such as large fishes, and the like; pigeons, and particularly the sort called smiters, have a way of clashing their wings the one against the other over their backs with a loud snap; another variety called tumblers turn themselves over in the air. Some birds have movements peculiar to the season of love: thus ring-doves, though strong and rapid at other times, yet in the spring hang about on the wing in a toying and playful manner; thus the cock-snipe, while breeding, forgetting his former flight, fans the air like the windhover; and the greenfinch in particular exhibits such languishing and faltering gestures as to appear like a wounded and dying bird; the kingfisher darts along like an arrow; fern-owls, or goat-suckers, glance in the dusk over the tops of trees like a meteor; starlings as it were swim along, while missel-thrushes use a wide and desultory flight; swallows sweep over the surface of the ground and water, and distinguish themselves by rapid turns and quick evolutions; swifts dash round in circles; and the bank-martin moves with frequent vacillations like a butterfly. Most of the small birds fly by jerks, rising and falling as they advance. Most small birds hop; but wagtails and larks walk, moving their legs alternately. Skylarks rise and fall perpendicularly as they sing; woodlarks hang poised in the air; and titlarks rise and fall in large curves, singing in their descent. The white-throat uses odd jerks and gesticulations over the tops of hedges and bushes. All the duck-kind waddle; divers and auks walk as if fettered, and stand erect on their tails; these are the *compedes* of Linnaeus. Geese and cranes, and most wildfowls, move in figured flights, often changing their position. The secondary remiges of *Tringae*, wild-ducks and some others, are very long, and give their wings, when in motion, an hooked appearance. Dabchicks, moorhens and coots, fly erect, with their legs hanging down, and hardly make any dispatch: the reason is plain, their wings are placed too forward out of the true centre of gravity; as the legs of auks and divers are situated too backwards."

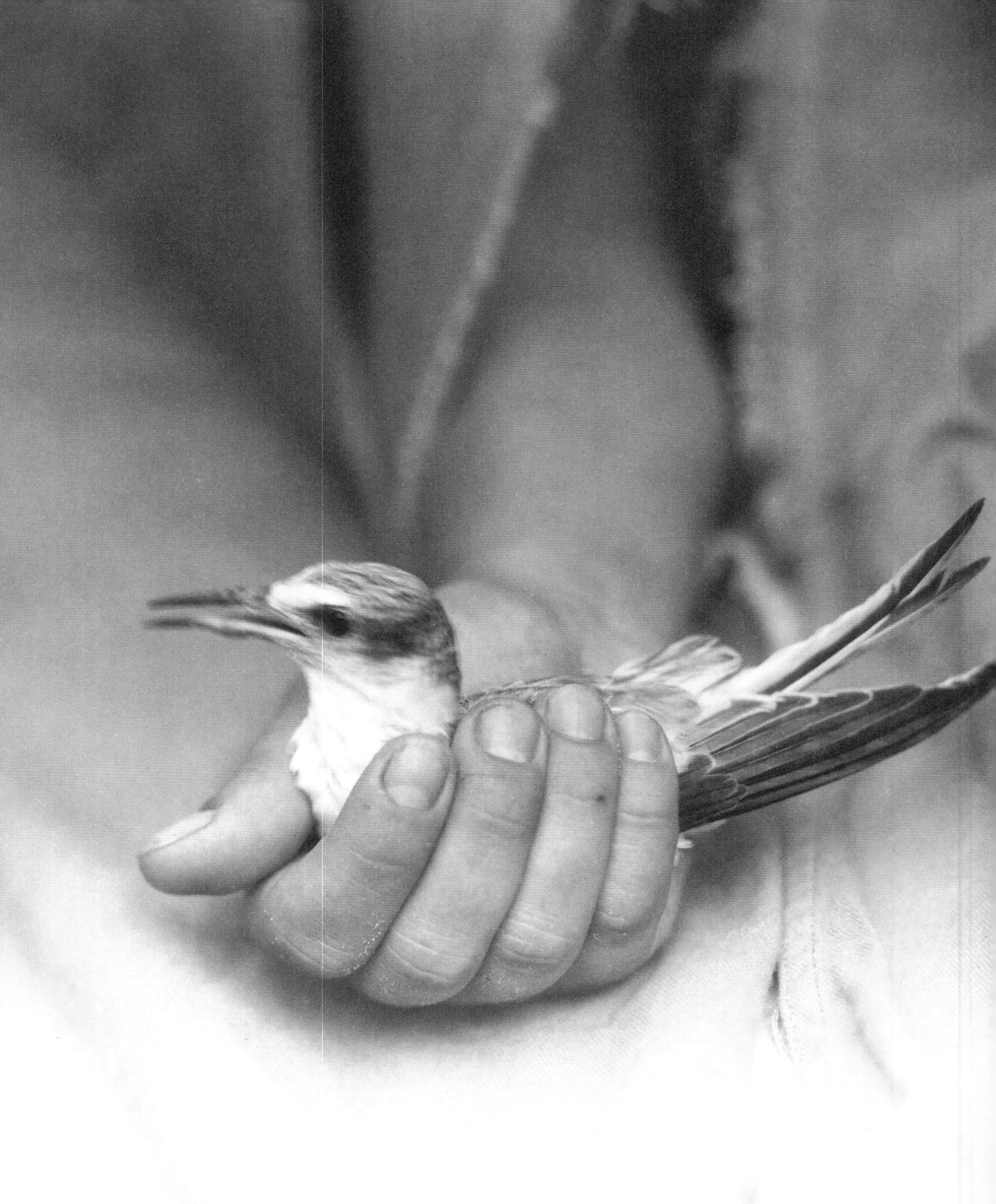

LEAST TERN

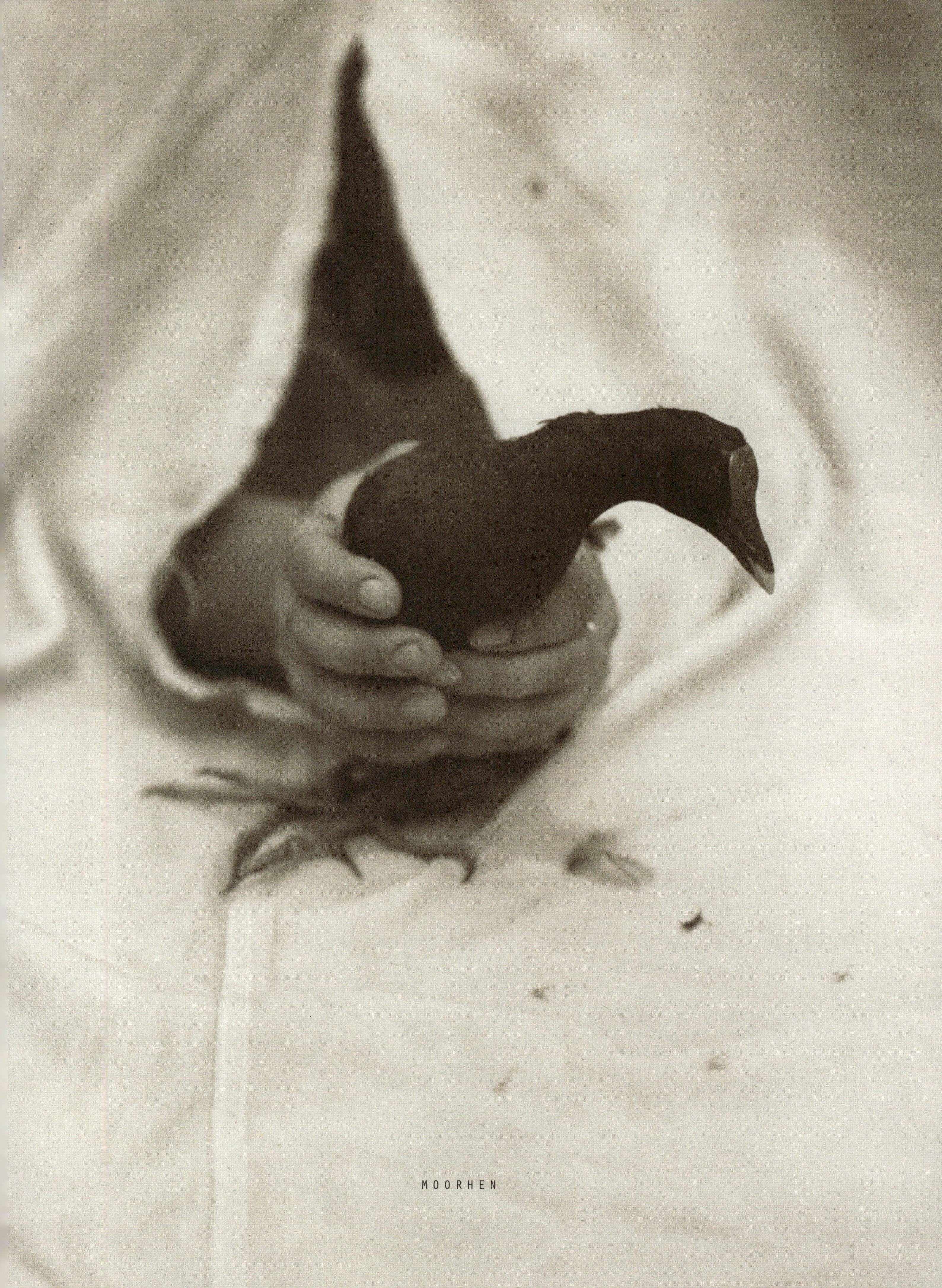

MOORHEN

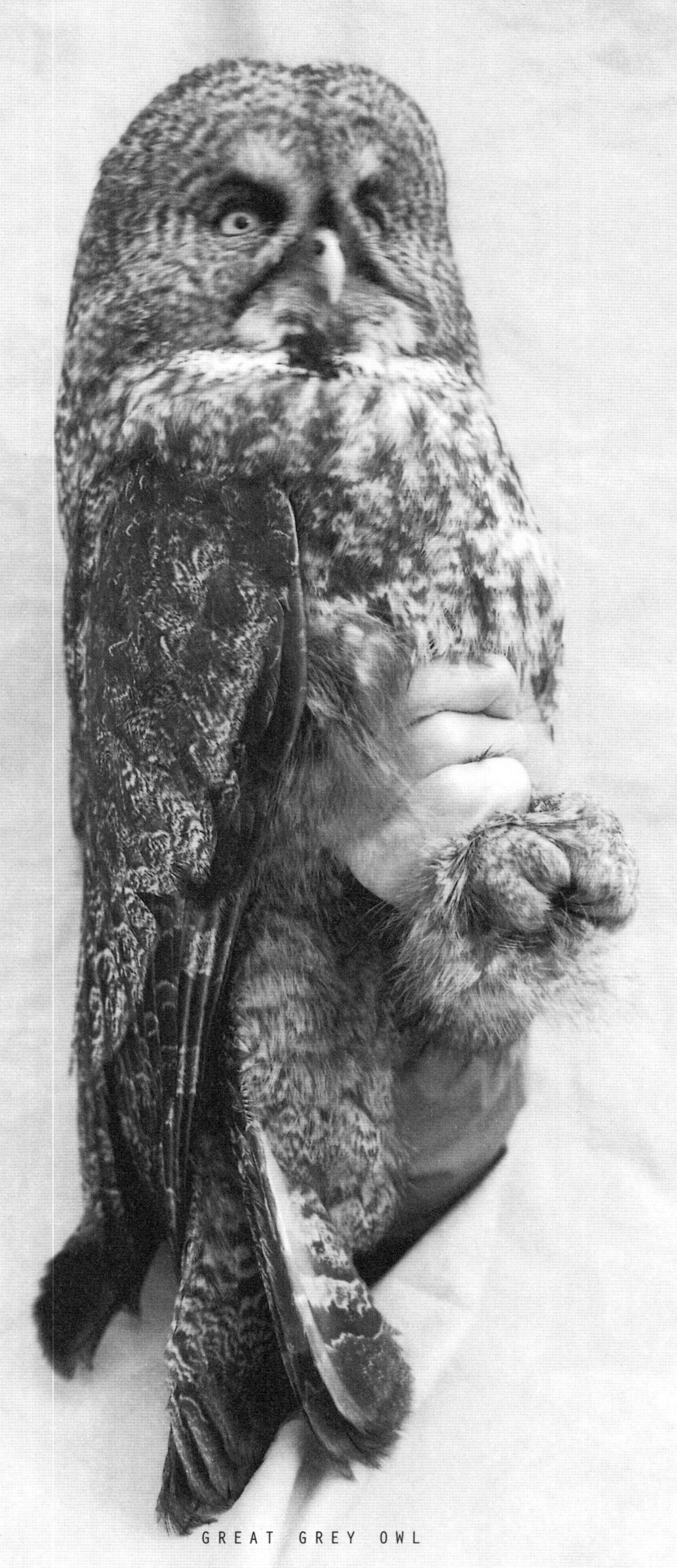

GREAT GREY OWL

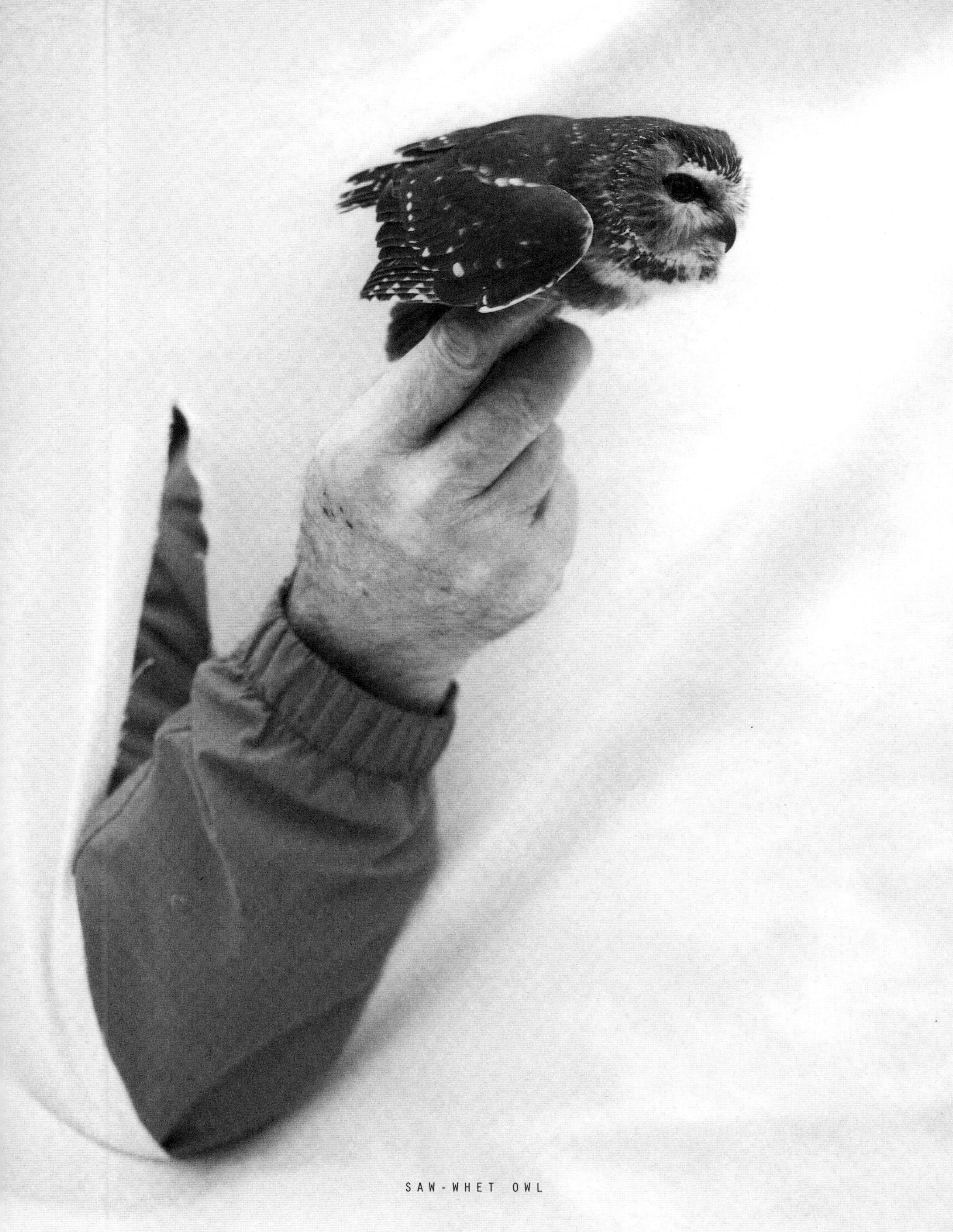

SAW-WHET OWL

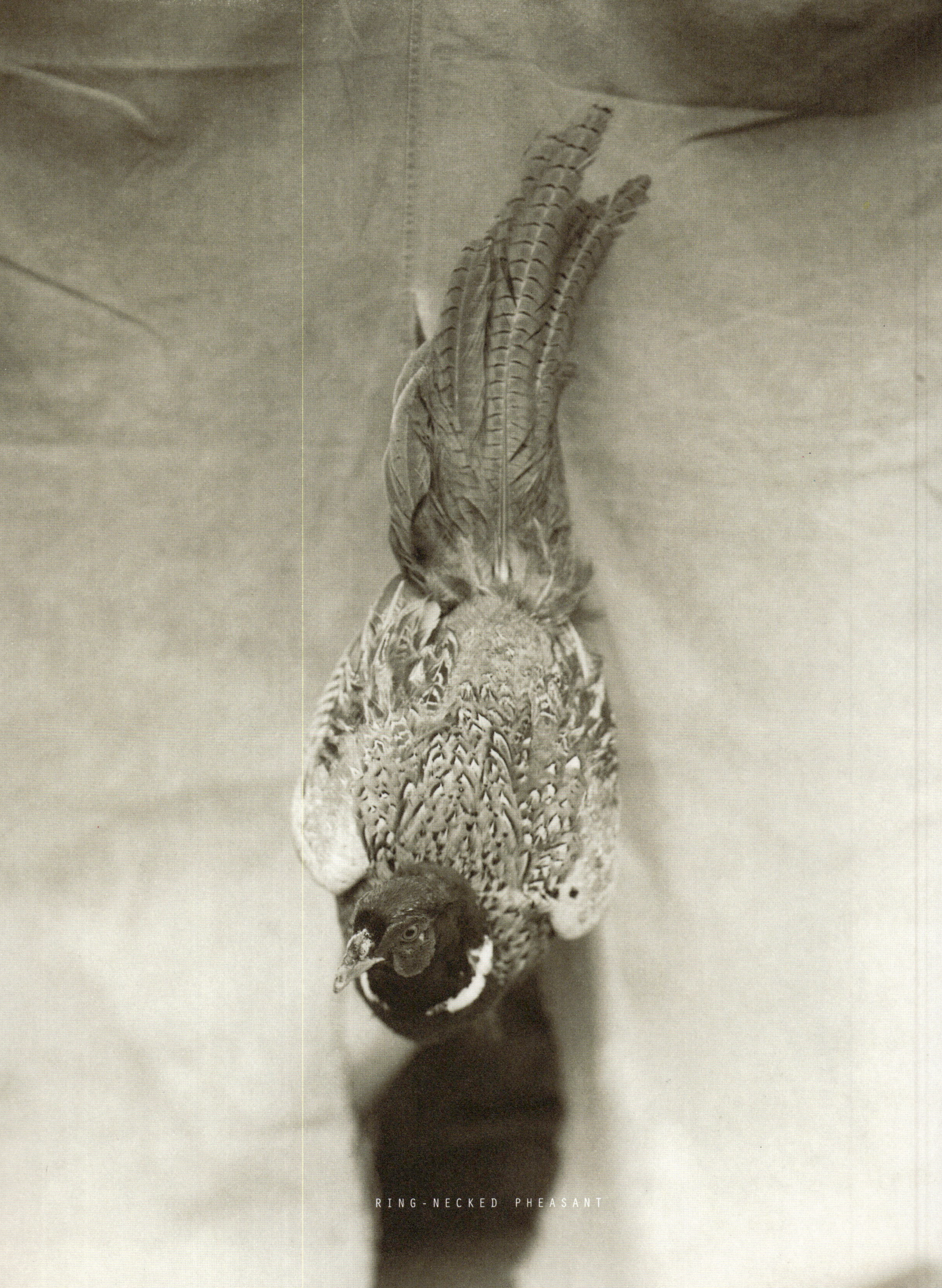

RING-NECKED PHEASANT

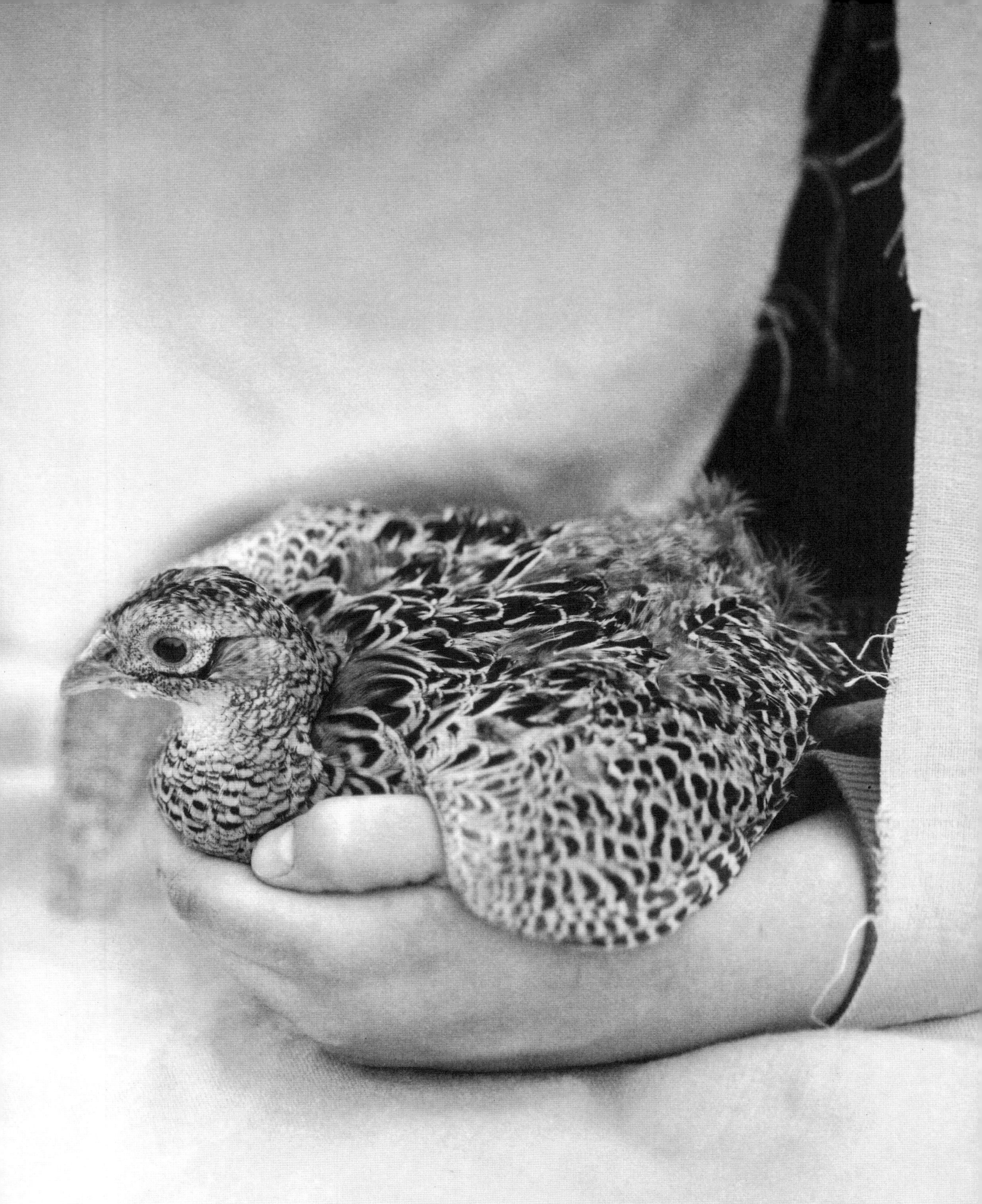

RING-NECKED PHEASANT

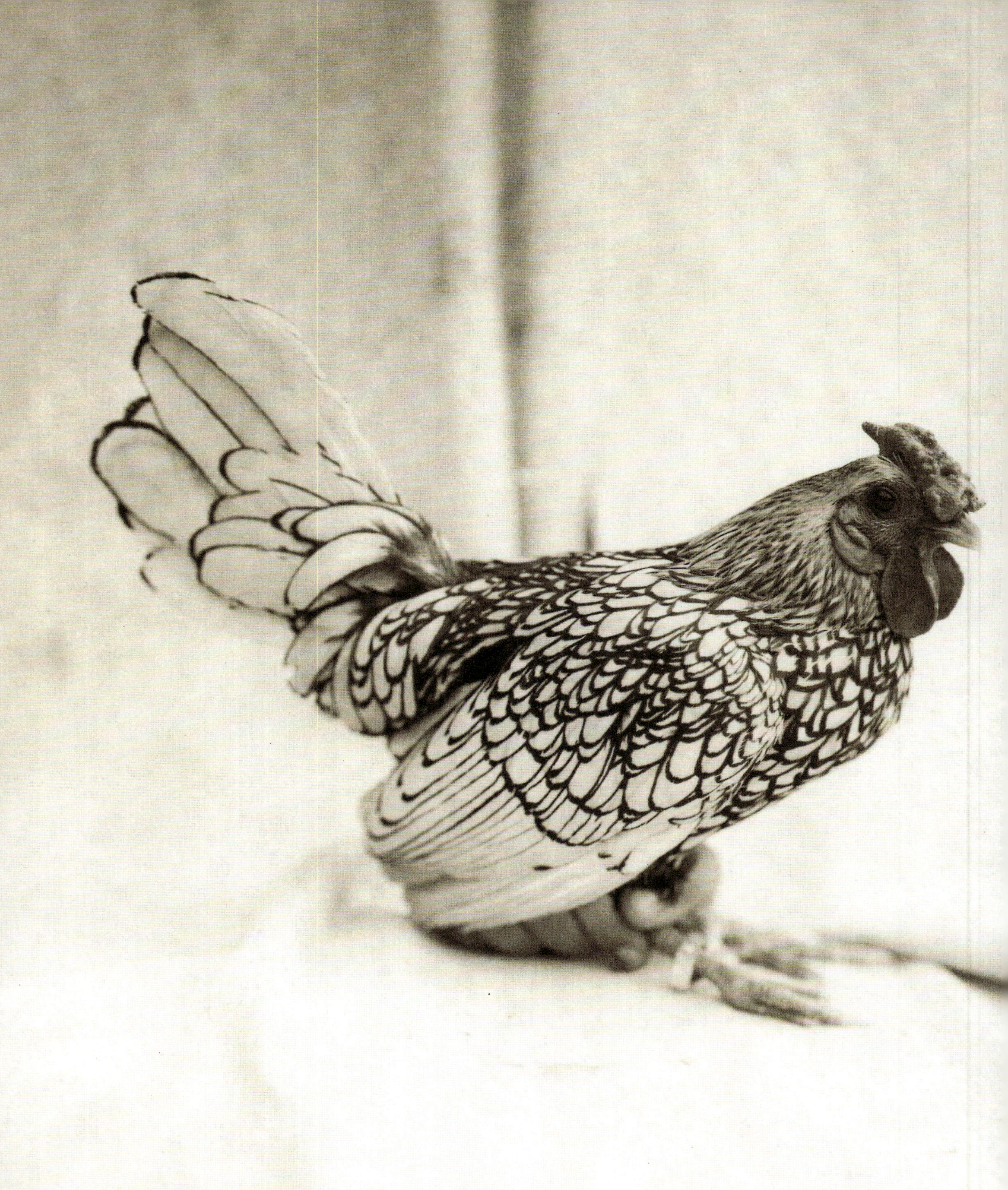

SILVER SEBRIGHT CHICKEN

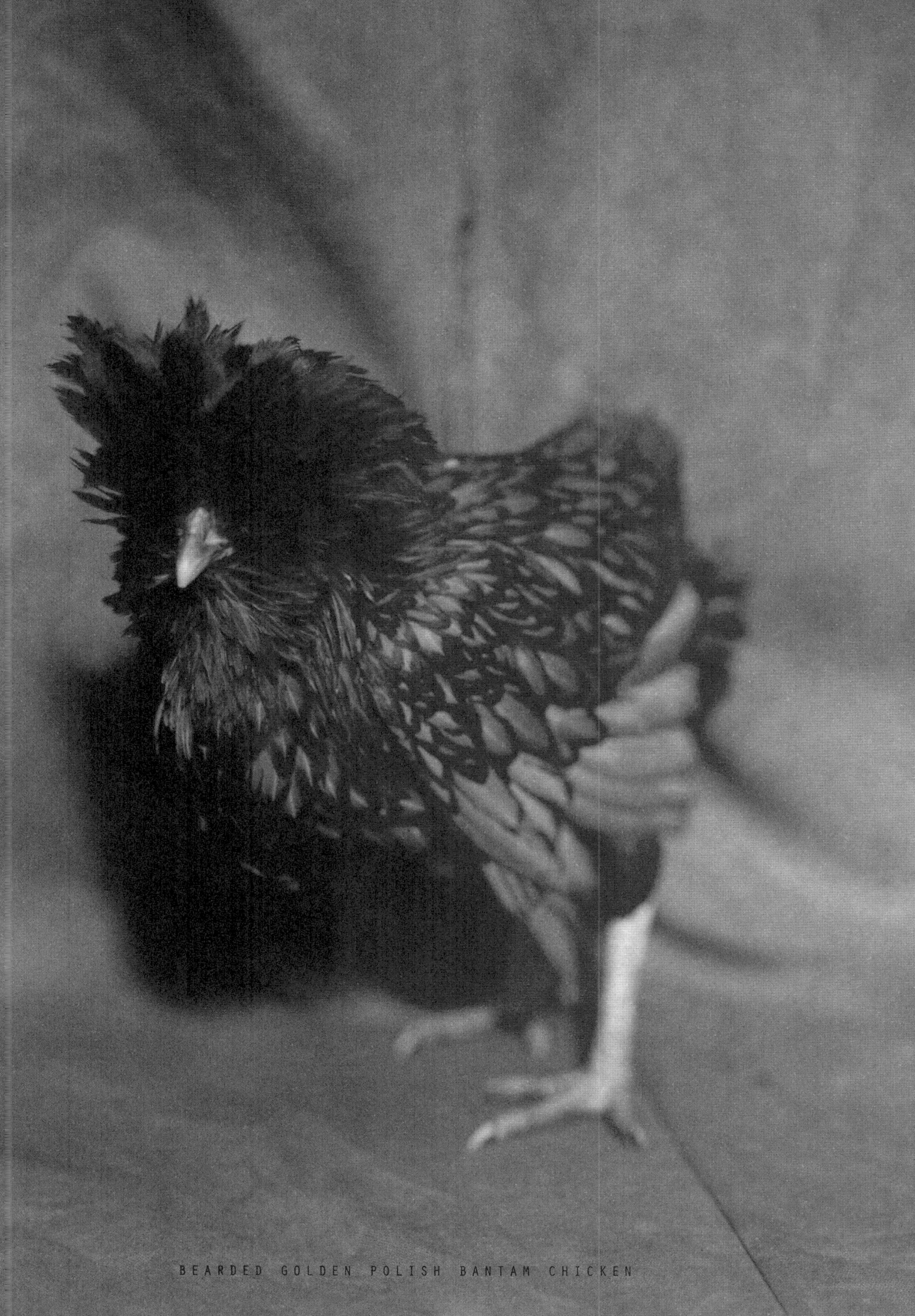

BEARDED GOLDEN POLISH BANTAM CHICKEN

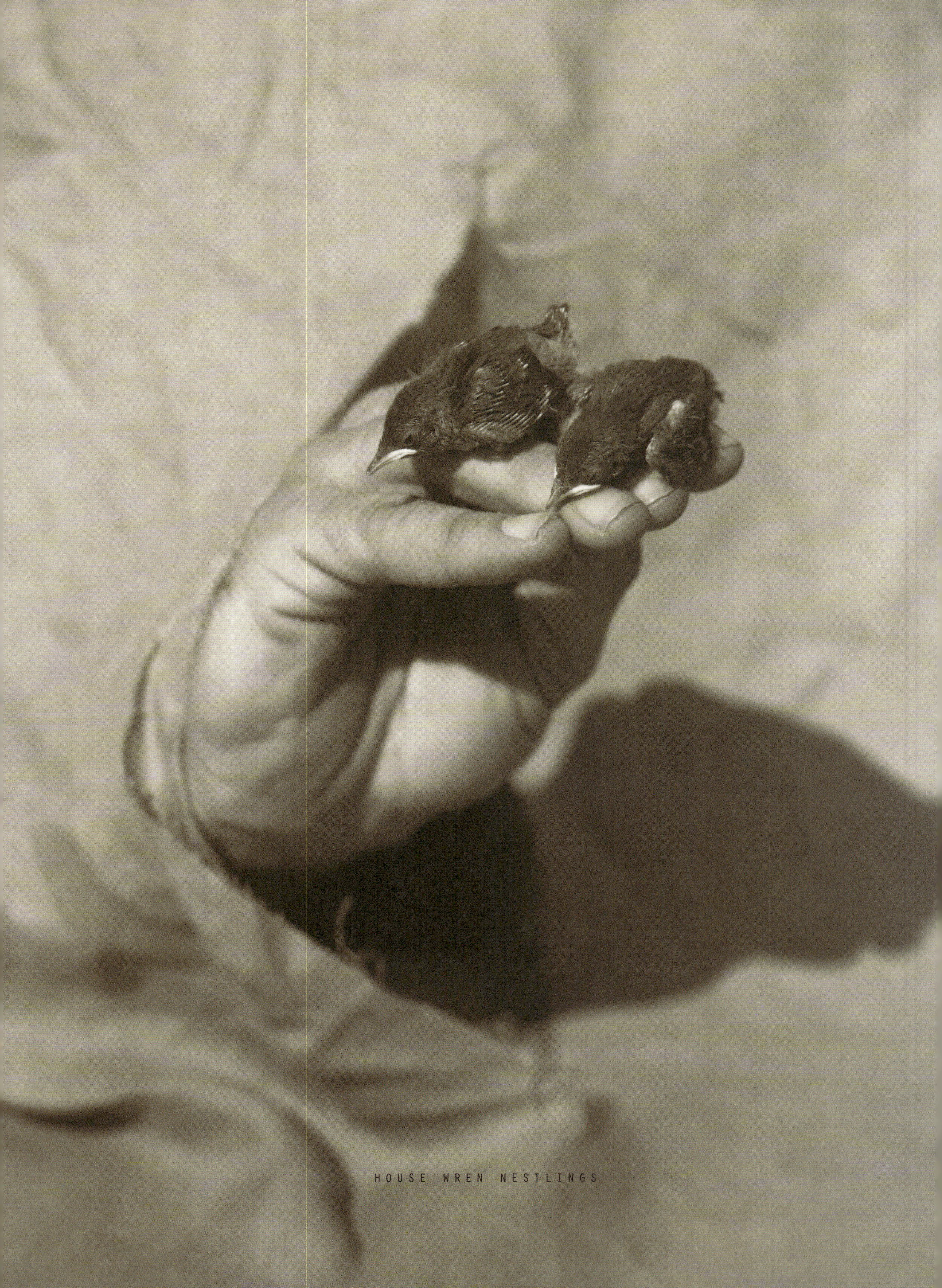

HOUSE WREN NESTLINGS

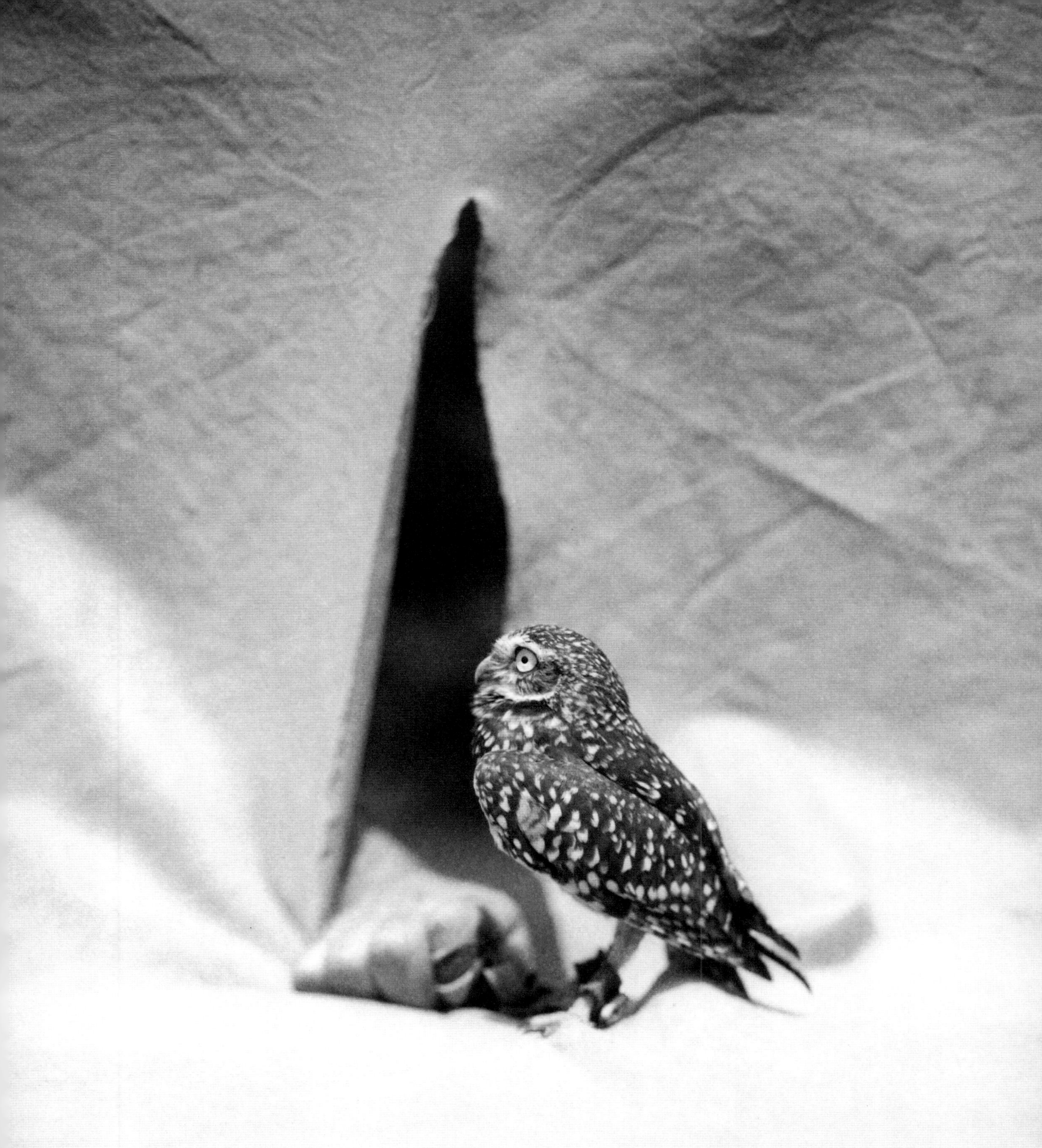

BURROWING OWL

Linnaeus constructed a taxonomy around variations in beak and claw. Charles Darwin studied variations in domesticated animals to test his theory of selection and gradual development of characteristics. He was particularly interested in pigeons, writing that he had kept every breed he could purchase or obtain, had "been most kindly favoured with skins from several quarters of the world" and with his usual thoroughness had "associated with several eminent fanciers and have been permitted to join two of the London Pigeon Clubs." His list of pigeons is science in the making, but the excitement of his observation, his passion, makes it as gripping as any poetry.

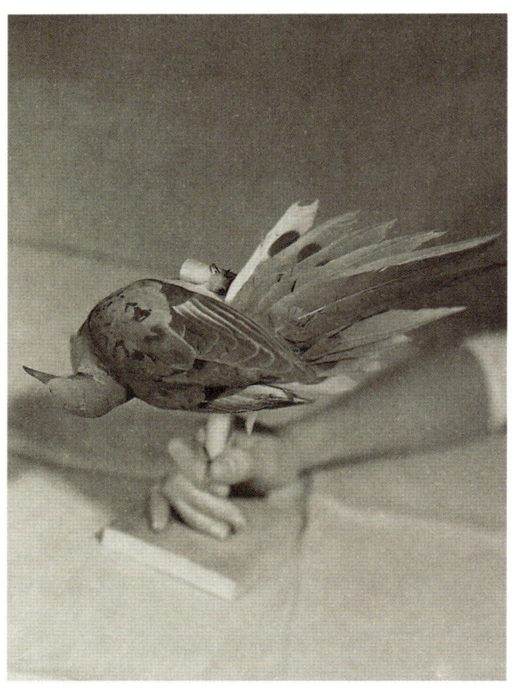

The diversity of the breeds is something astonishing. Compare the English carrier and the short-faced tumbler, and see the wonderful difference in their beaks, entailing corresponding differences in their skulls. The carrier, more especially the male bird, is also remarkable from the wonderful development of the carunculated skin about the head, and this is accompanied by greatly elongated eyelids, very large external orifices to the nostrils, and a wide gape of mouth. The short-faced tumbler has a beak in outline almost like that of a finch; and the common tumbler has the singular inherited habit of flying at a great height in a compact flock, and tumbling in the air head over heels. The runt is a bird of great size, with long massive beak, large feet; some of the sub-breeds of runt have very long necks, others very long wings and tails, others singularly short tails. The barb is allied to the carrier, but, instead of a very long beak, has a very short and very broad one. The pouter has a much elongated body, wings and legs; and its enormously developed crop, which it glories in inflating, may well excite astonishment and even laughter. The turbit has a very short and conical beak, with a line of

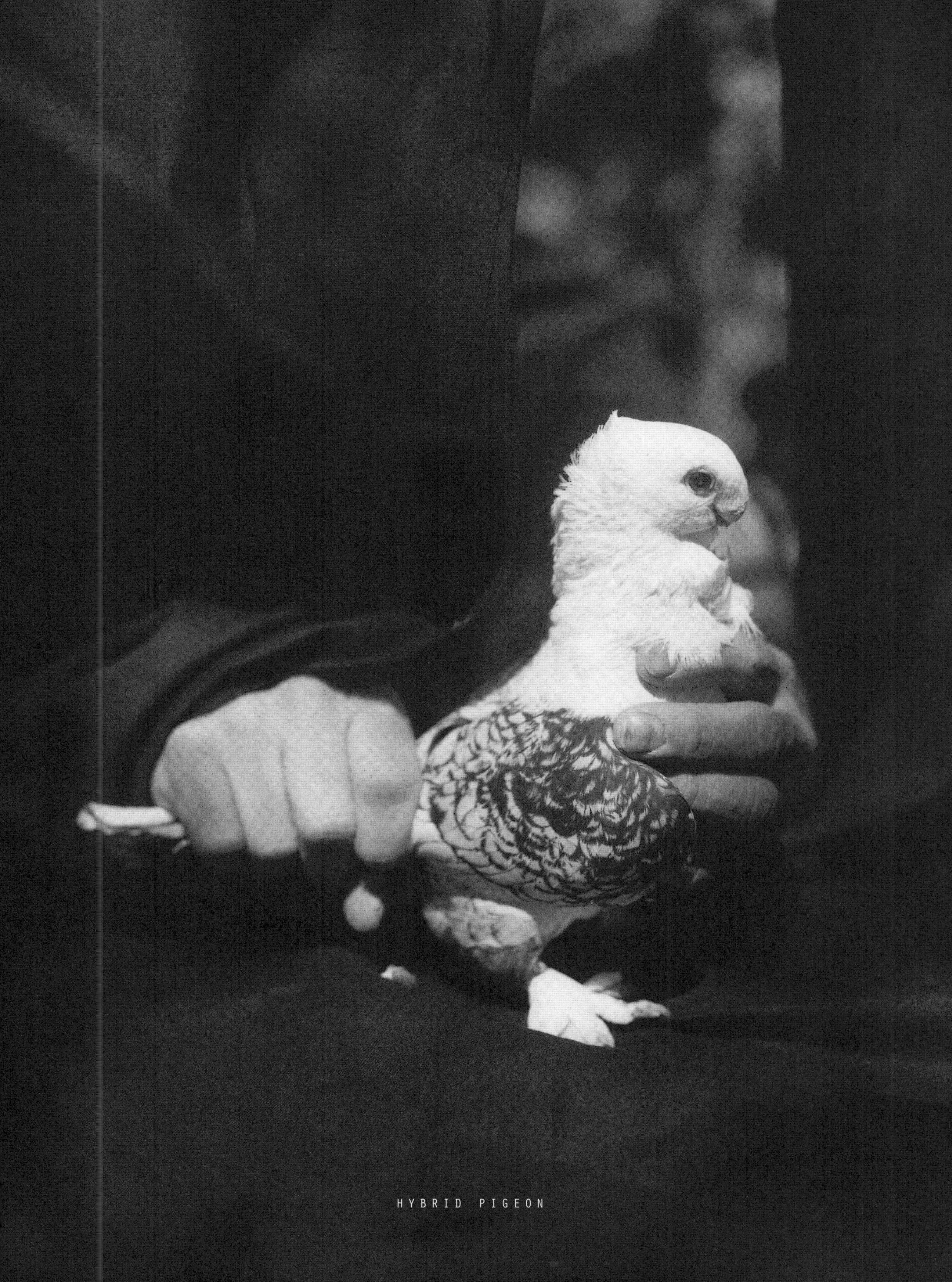

HYBRID PIGEON

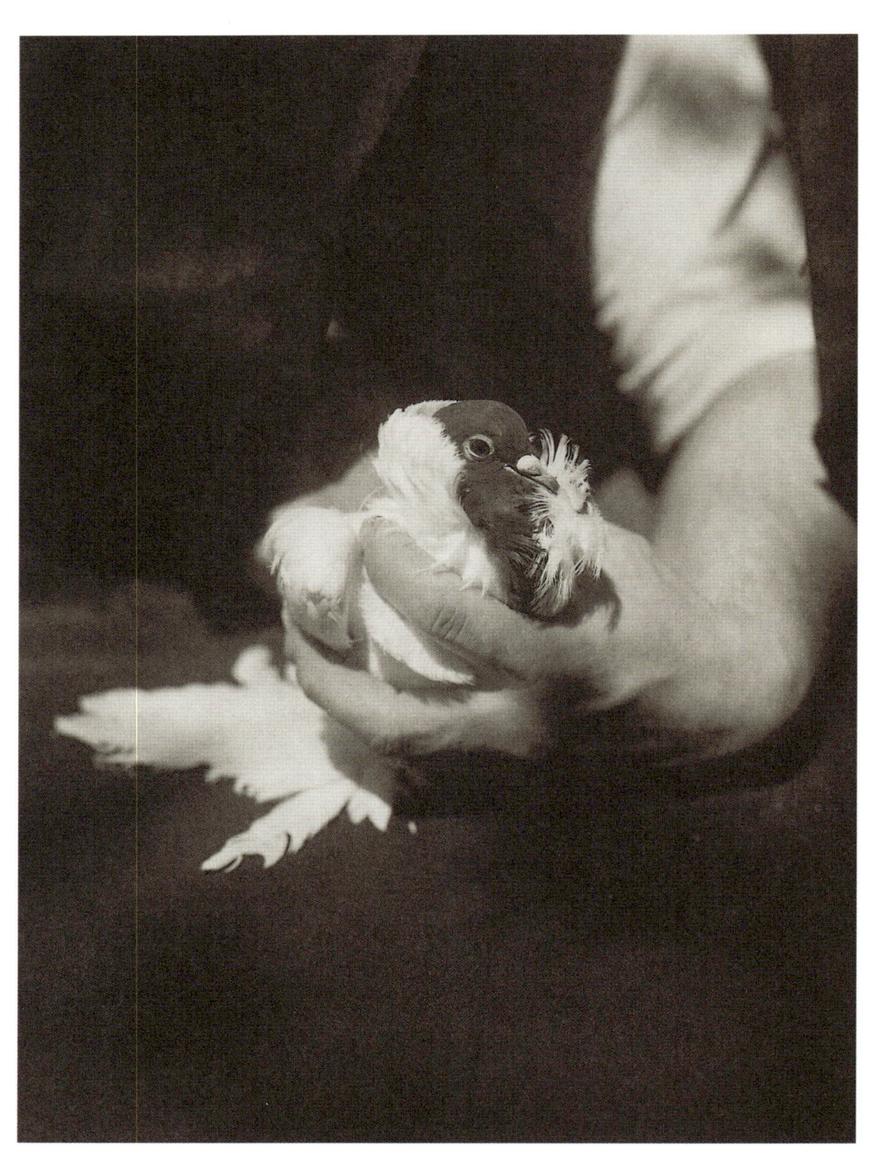

HYBRID PIGEON

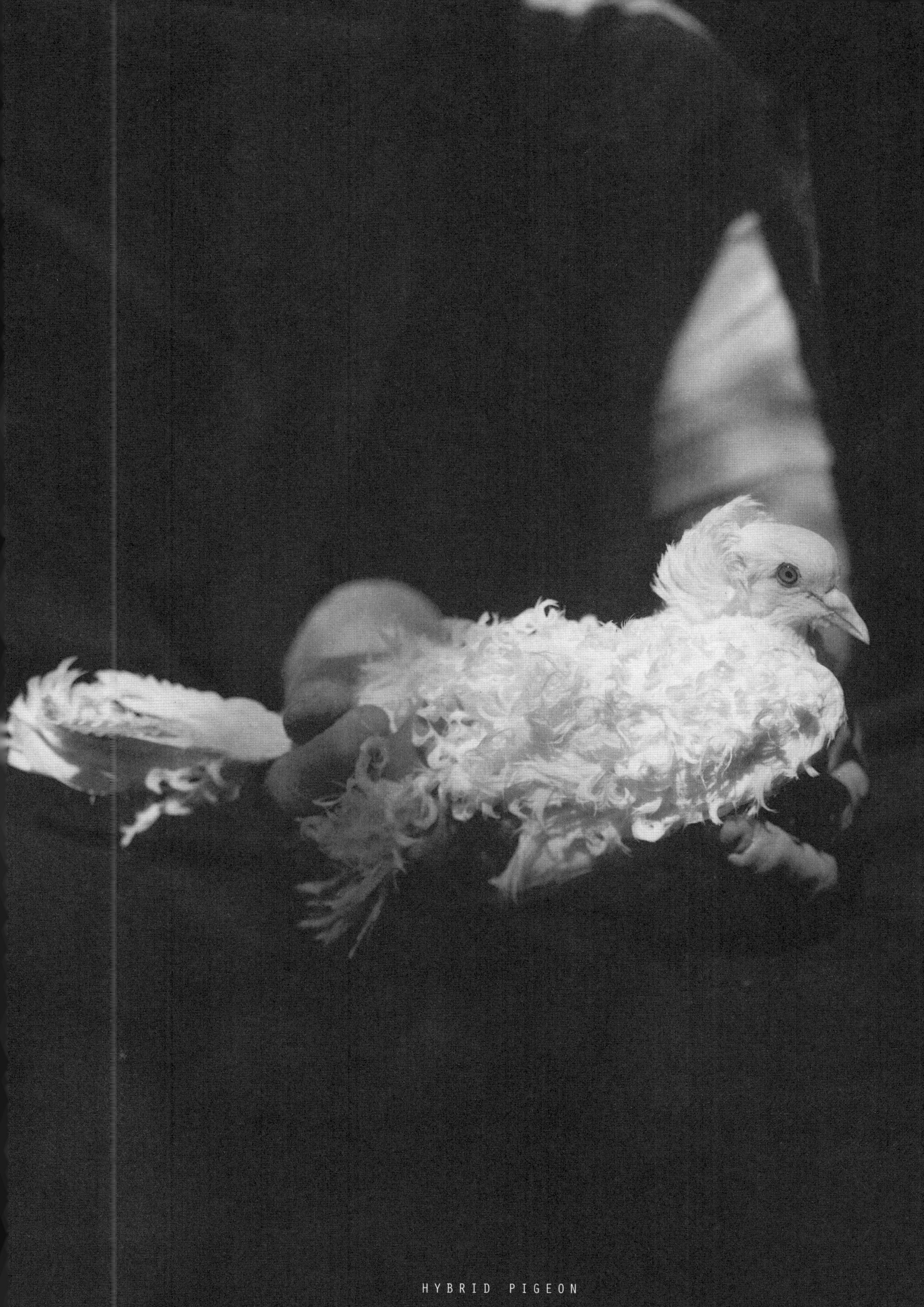

HYBRID PIGEON

reversed feathers down the breast; and it has the habit of continually expanding slightly the upper part of the oesophagus. The Jacobin has the feathers so much reversed along the back of the neck that they form a hood, and it has, proportionately to its size, much elongated wing and tail feathers. The trumpeter and laughter [sic.], as their names express, utter a very different coo from the other breeds. The fantail has thirty or even forty tail feathers, instead of the twelve or fourteen, the normal number in all members of the great pigeon family; and these feathers are kept expanded, and carried so erect, that in good birds the head and tail touch; the oil-gland is quite aborted. Several other less distinct breeds might be specified.

In the skeletons of the several breeds, the development of the bones of the face in length and breadth and curvature differs enormously. The shape, as well as the breadth and length of the ramus of the lower jaw, varies in a highly remarkable manner. The number of caudal and sacral vertebrae vary; as does the number of the ribs, together with their relative breadth and the presence of processes. The size and shape of the apertures in the sternum are highly variable; so is the degree of divergence and relative size of the two arms of the furcula. The proportional width of the gape of mouth, the proportional length of the eyelids, of the orifice of the nostrils, of the tongue, (not always in strict correlation with the length of beak), the size of the crop and of the upper part of the oesophagus; the development and abortion of the oil-gland; the number of the primary wing and caudal feathers; the relative length of wing and tail to each other and to the body; the relative length of leg and of the feet; the number of scutellae on the toes, the development of skin between the toes, are all points of structure which are variable. The period at which the perfect plumage is acquired varies, as does the state of the down with which the nestling birds are clothed when hatched. The shape and size of the eggs vary. The manner of flight differs remarkably; as does in some breeds the voice and disposition. Lastly in certain breeds the males and females have come to differ to a slight degree from each other.

Altogether at least a score of pigeons might be chosen, which, if shown to an ornithologist, and he were told that they were wild birds, would certainly, I think, be ranked by him as well-defined species. Moreover, I do not believe that any ornithologist would place the English carrier, the short-faced tumbler, the runt, the barb, pouter, and fantail in the same genus; more especially as in each of these breeds several truly inherited sub-breeds, or species as he would call them could be shown him.

Great as the differences are between the breeds of pigeons, I am fully convinced that the common opinion of naturalists is correct, namely, that all have descended from the rock-pigeon (Columba livia).

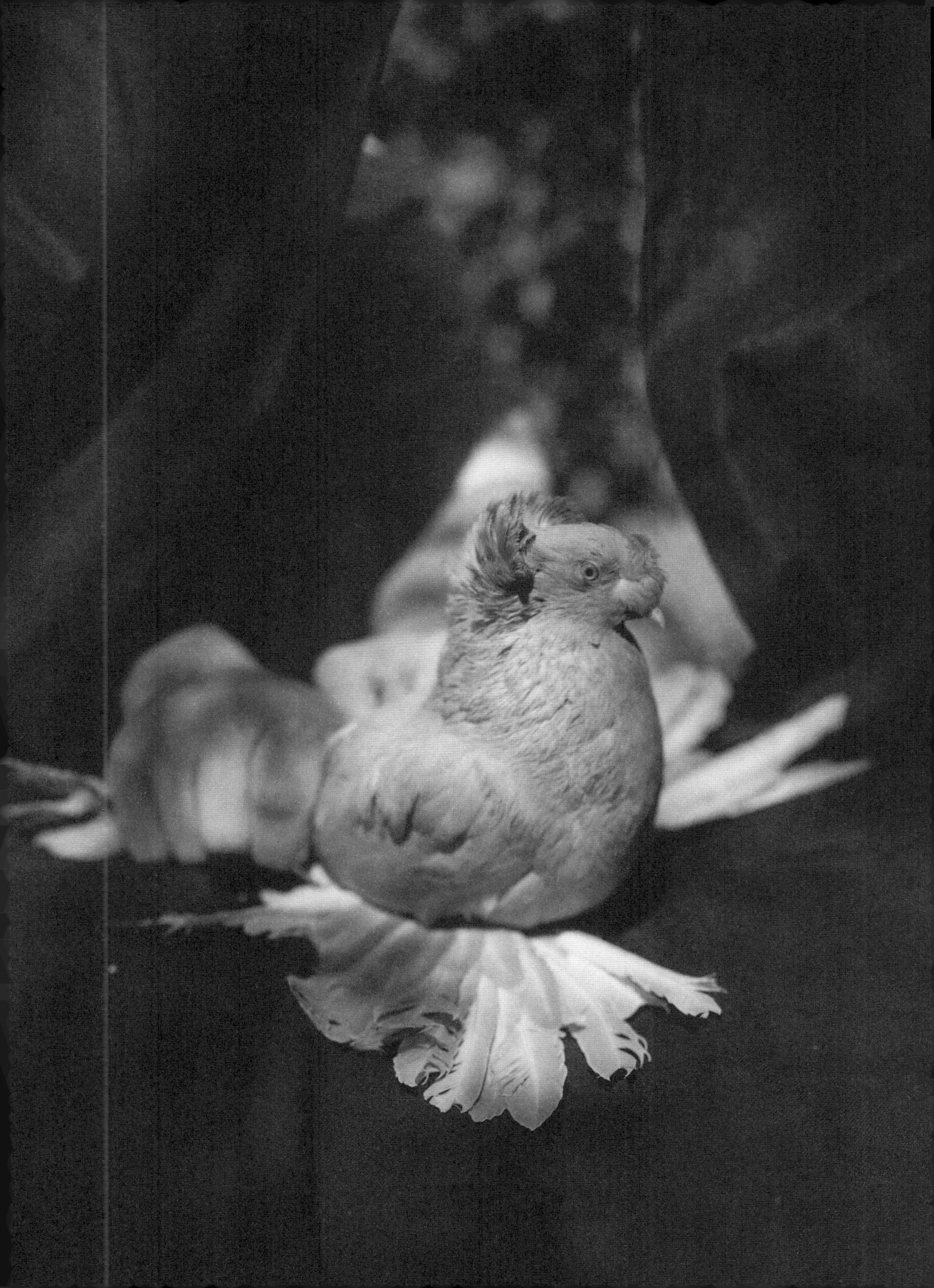

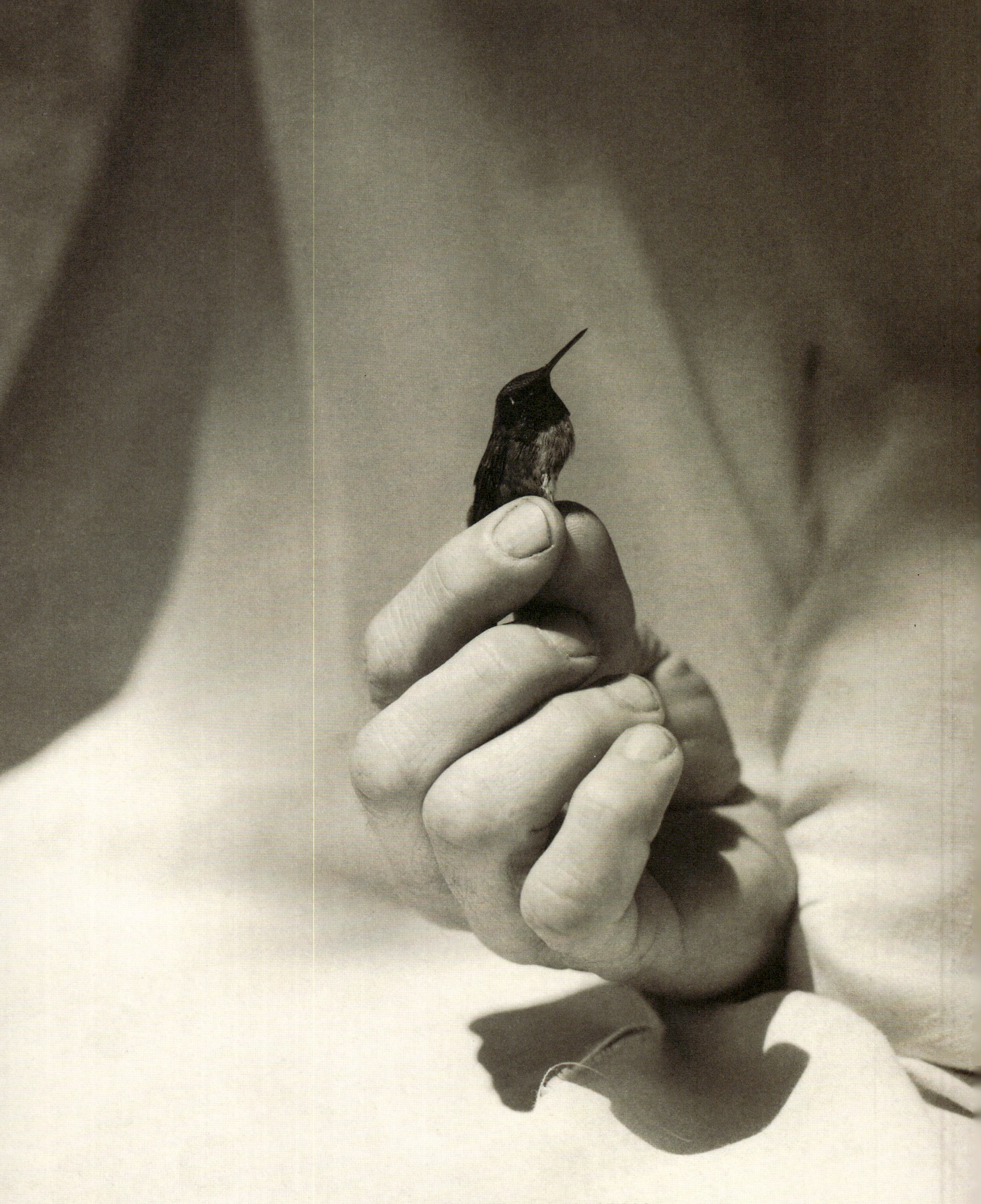

RUBY-THROATED HUMMINGBIRD

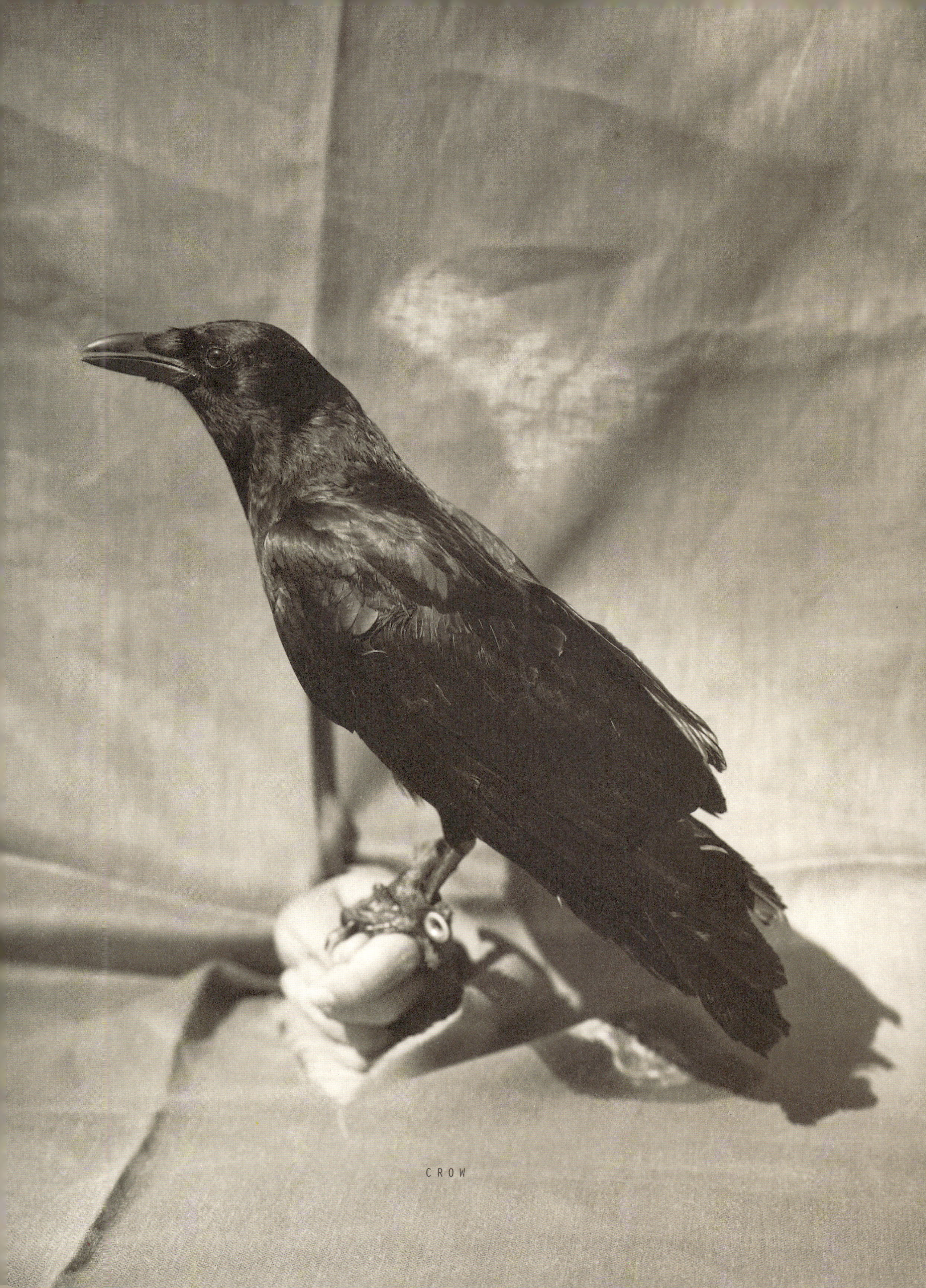

CROW

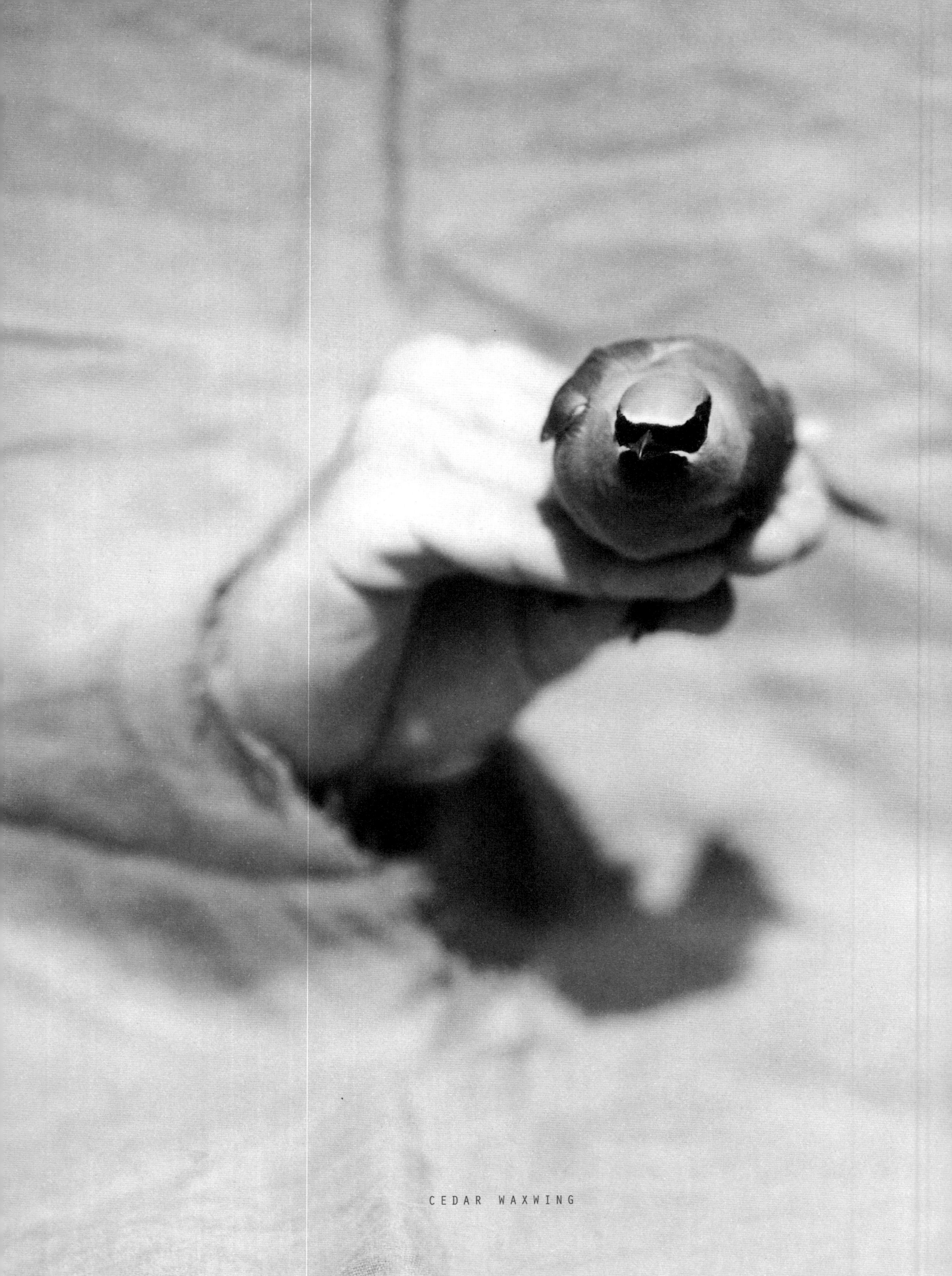

CEDAR WAXWING

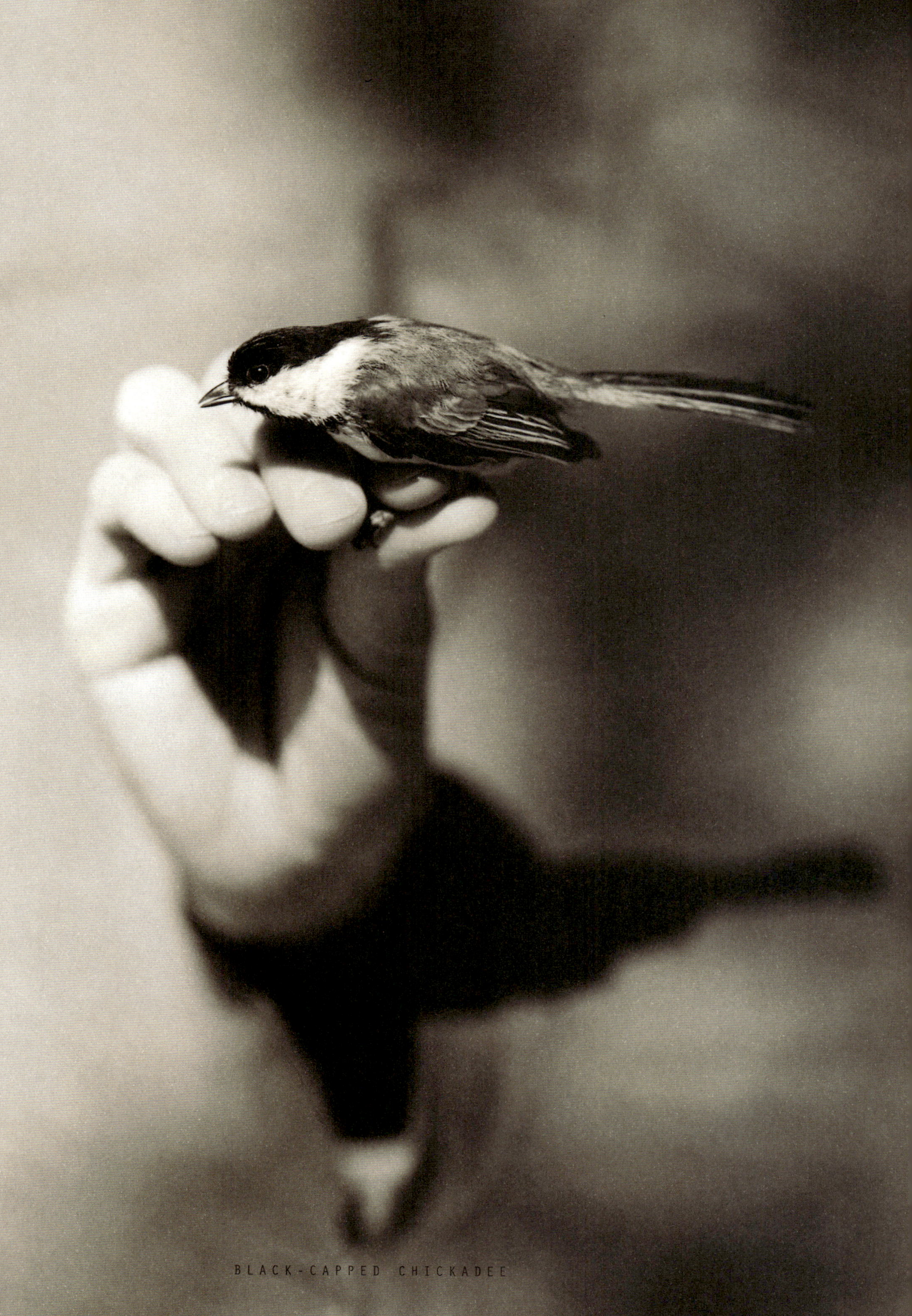

BLACK-CAPPED CHICKADEE

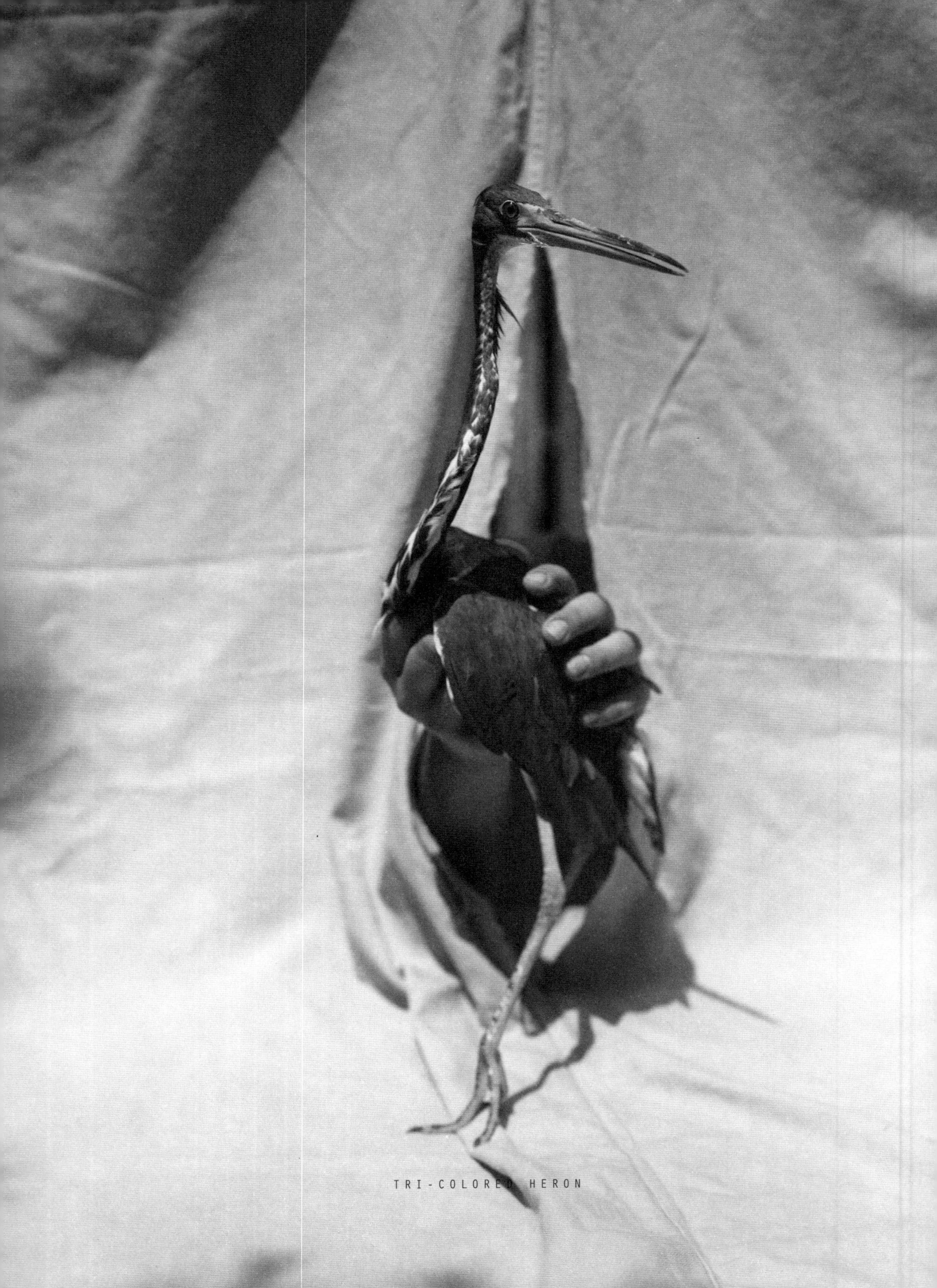

TRI-COLORED HERON

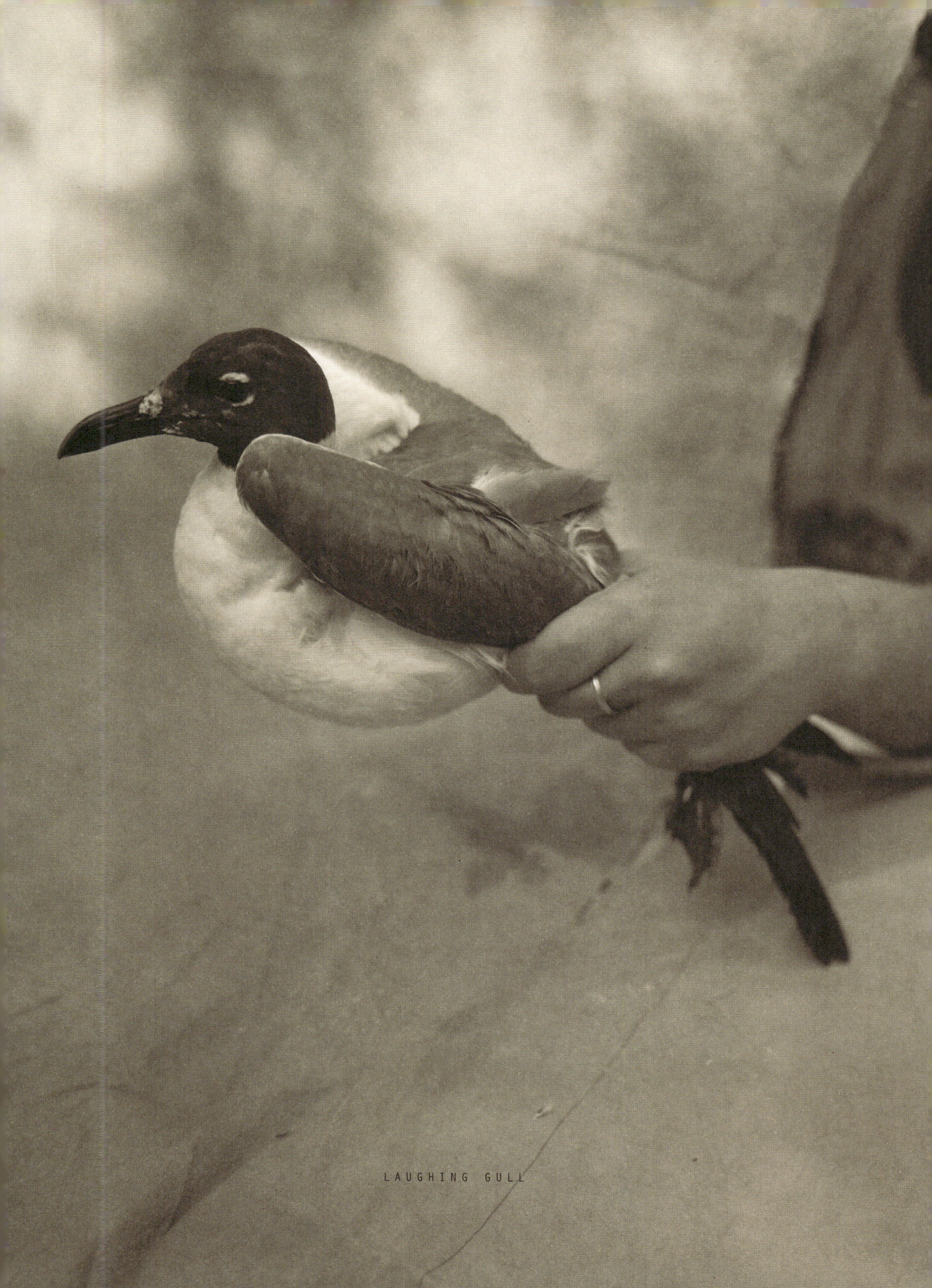

LAUGHING GULL

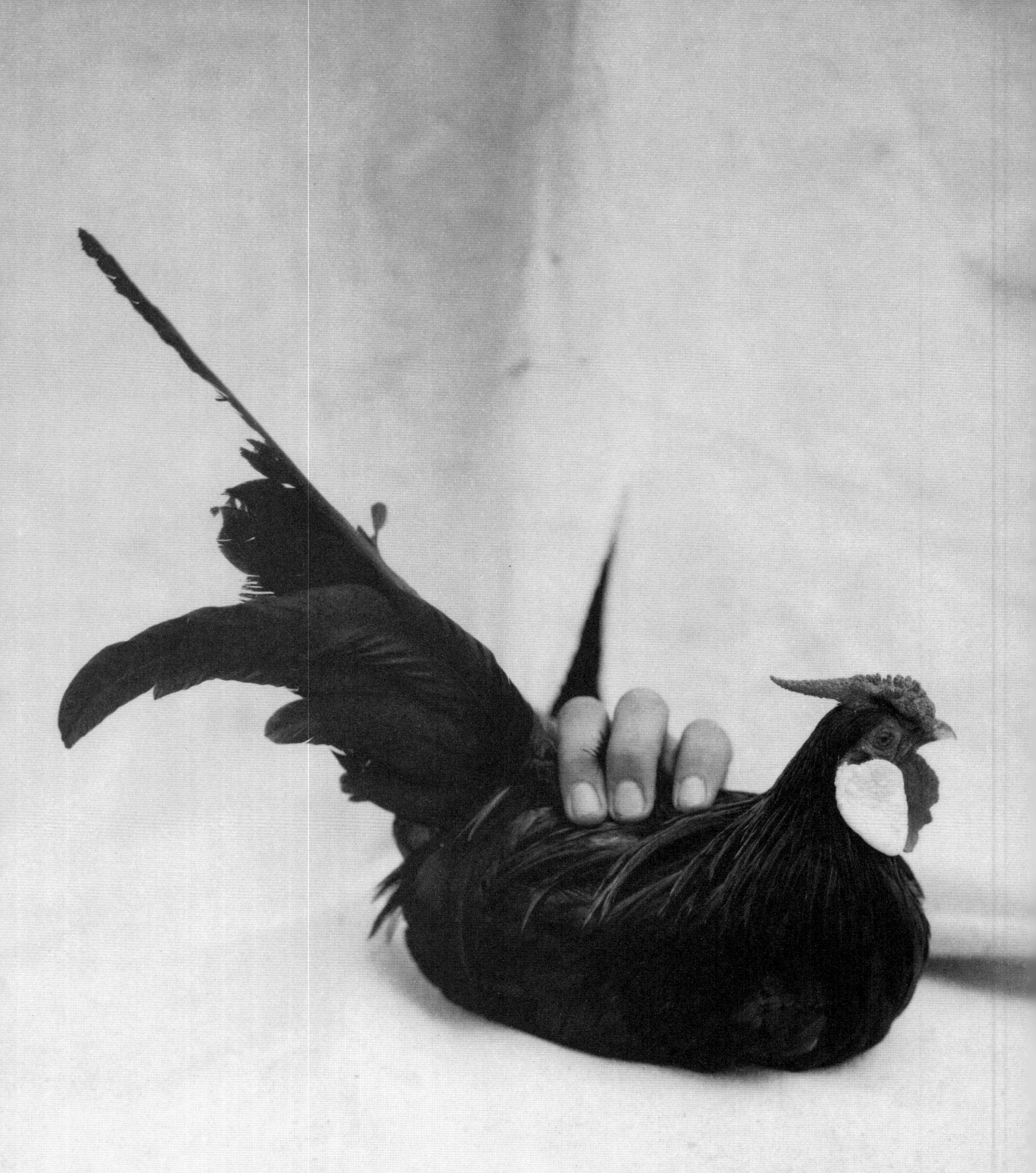

BLACK ROSECOMB CHICKEN

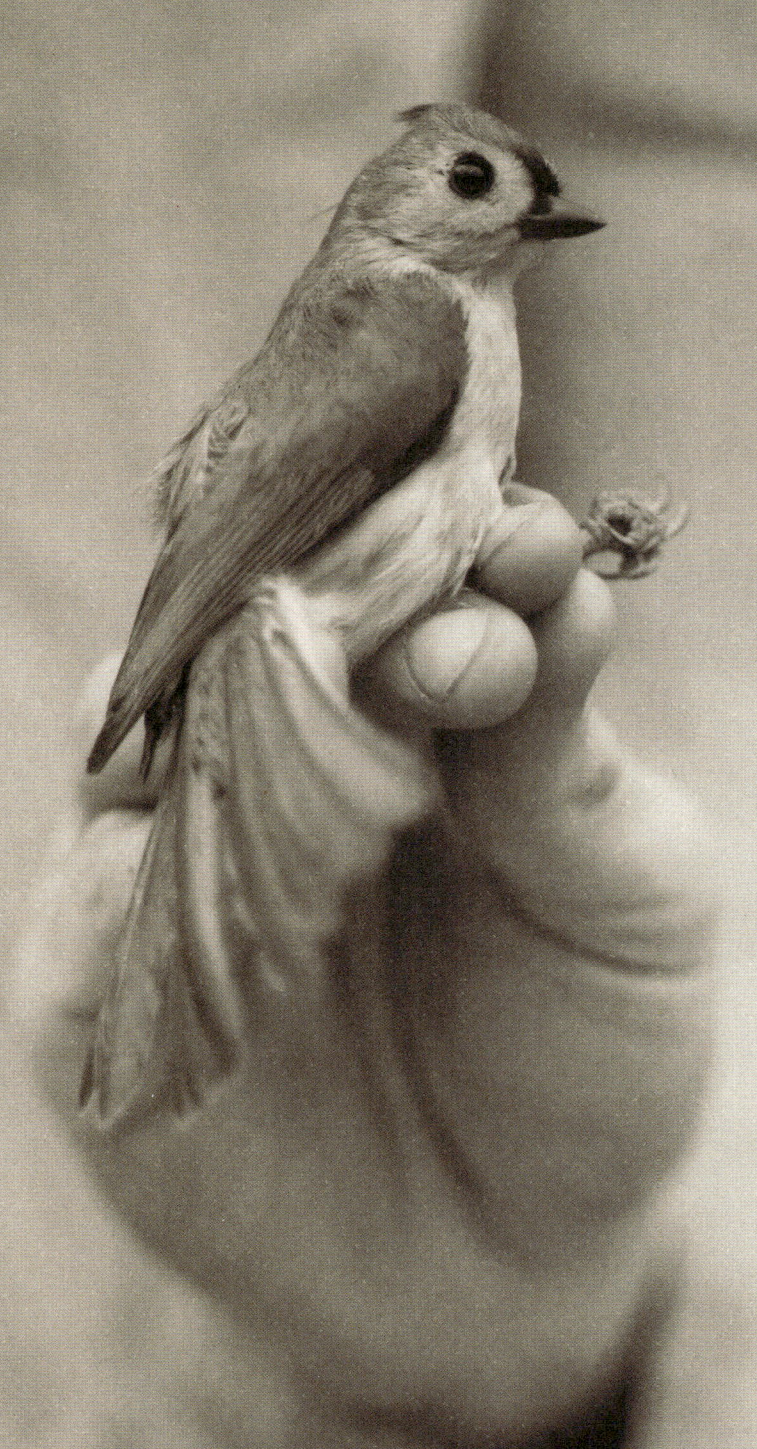

TUFTED TITMOU[illegible]

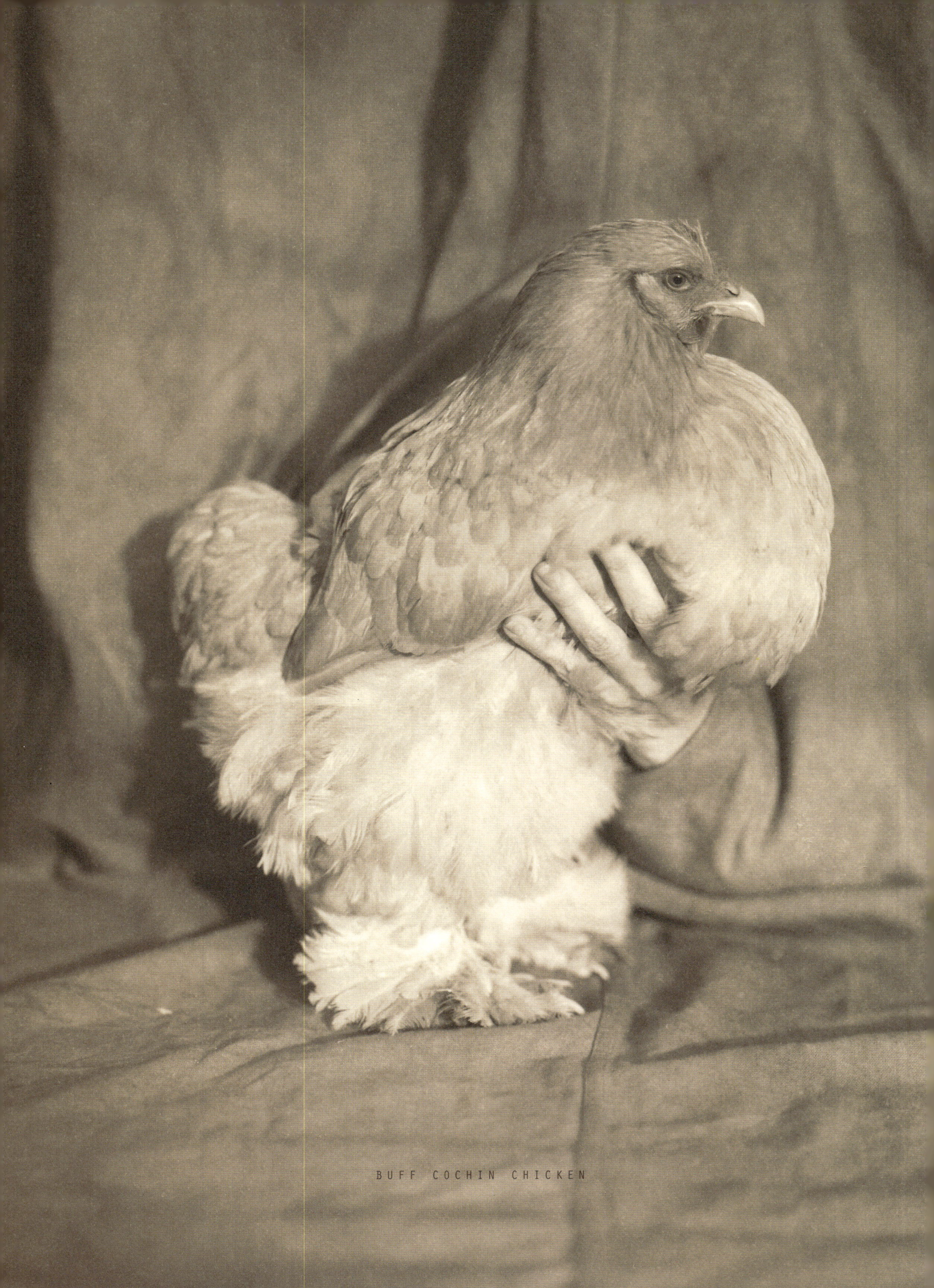

BUFF COCHIN CHICKEN

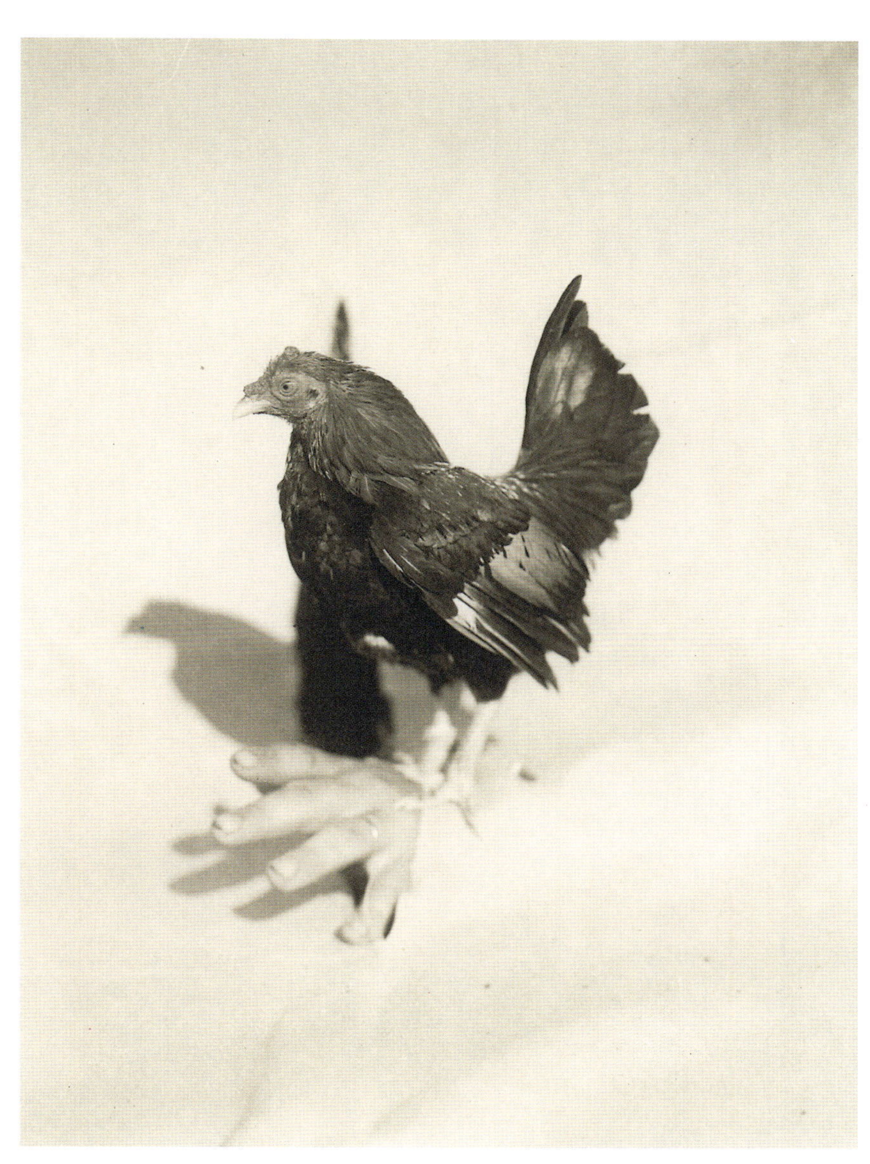

OLD ENGLISH SILVER DUCKWING GAME BANTAM CHICKEN

Darwin's attention to bone, beak, and feather is a form of intense relation to the birds, and Darwin's theories of natural selection and development of species connected human beings with the creatures in ways it took a long time, and the discoveries of the geneticists of our own time, for human beings to be able to imagine. The objective eye of the scientist revealed a kinship in and under the skin, in the eye itself. But the twentieth century produced anxieties about our relations with the creatures, about the casual killing and collecting which came both from our inheritance as unthinking subsistence hunters and farmers, and also from the distance produced by urban life, human proliferation, the habit of study. W.H. Hudson [1841–1922], the naturalist, wrote most imaginatively about the lives of birds, both in the tropics and in the English countryside which was changing rapidly during his lifetime. He wrote on migration and on bird-song; he wrote about "Goldfinches at Ryme Intrinseca," "The furze-wren or furze-fairy," and "The strange and beautiful sheldrake." He wrote with precise sentimentality, to pull at the emotions, but to pull at them with unknown details of bird-life. He prefaces his *Birds and Man* (1901) with an impassioned expression of distaste for stuffed birds, then a fashionable decoration. He does not, he says, mind the birdskin collections of serious ornithologists, but

"The unpleasantness in the sight of skins stuffed with wool and set up on their legs in imitation of the living bird, sometimes (oh mockery!) in their 'natural surroundings.' These 'surroundings' are as a rule constructed or composed of a few handfuls of earth to form the floor of the glass case—sand, rock, clay, chalk, or gravel; whatever the material may be, it invariably has, like all matter 'out of place,' a grimy and depressing appearance. On the floor are planted grasses, sedges, and miniature bushes, made of tin or zinc and then dipped in a bucket of green paint. [I wrote once,] "When the eye closes in death, the bird, except to the naturalist, becomes a mere bundle of dead feathers; crystal globes may be put into the empty sockets, and a bold, life-imitating attitude given to the stuffed specimen, but the vitreous orbs shoot forth no lifelike glances: the 'passion and the fire whose fountains are within' have vanished, and the best work of the taxidermist, who has given a life to his bastard art, produces in the mind only sensations of irritation and disgust."

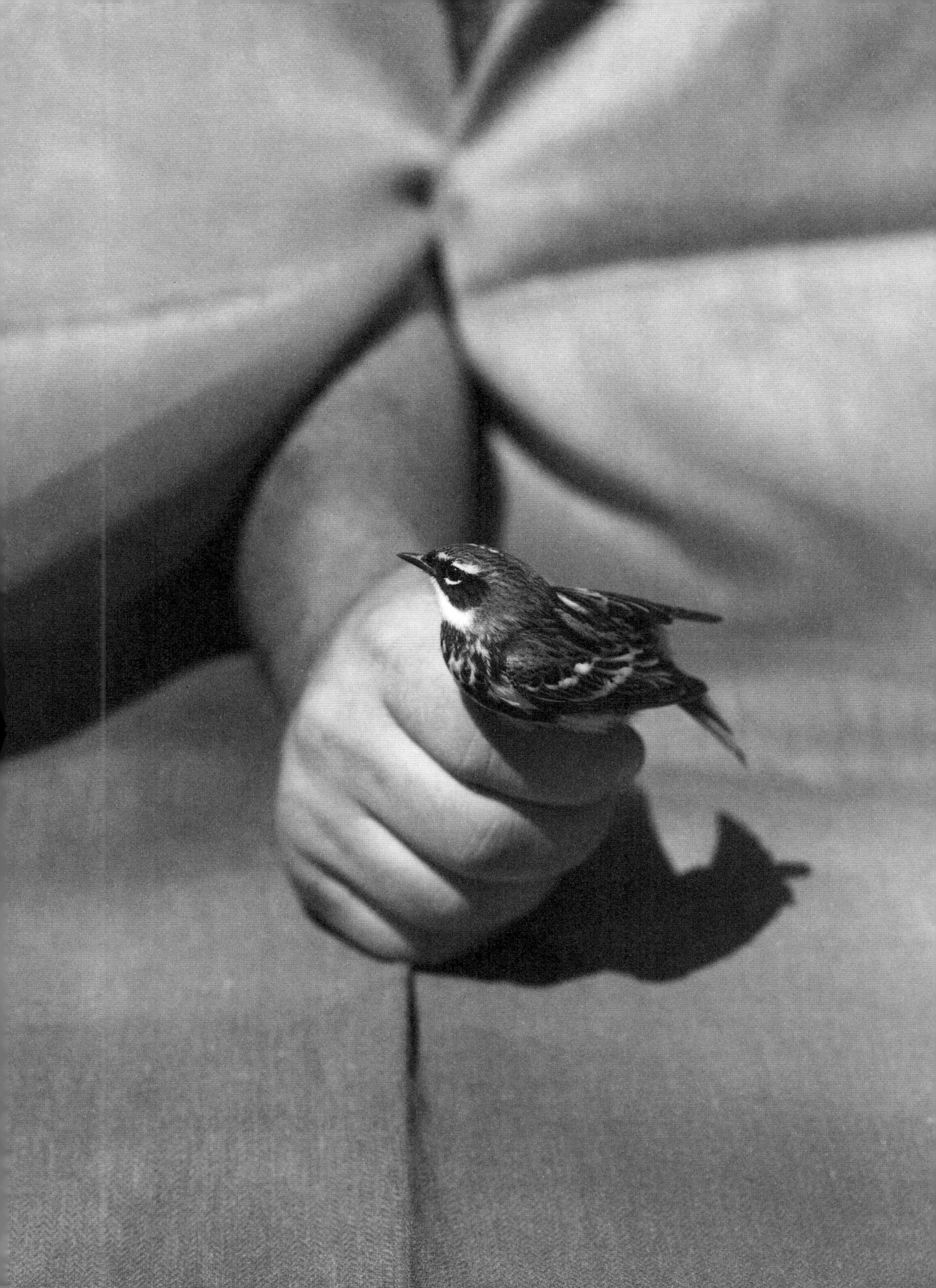

Here, by contrast, is Hudson at work observing mocking-birds, very much alive, and not always wholly delightful, separate, and interesting.

"The most curious example of true mimicry I have yet met with is that of a true mocking-bird, *Mimus patachonicus*, a common resident species in northern Patagonia, on the Atlantic side, very abundant in places. He is a *true* mocking-bird because he belongs to the genus Mimus, a branch of the thrush family, and not because he mocks or mimics the songs of other species like others of his kindred. He does not, in fact, mimic the set songs of others, although he often introduces notes and phrases borrowed from other species into his own performance. He sings in a sketchy way all the year round, but in spring has a fuller, unbroken song, emitted with more power and passion. For the rest of the time he sings to amuse himself, as it seems, in a peculiarly leisurely and one may say indolent manner, perched on a bush, from time to time emitting a note or two, then a phrase which, if it pleases him, he will repeat two or three or half a dozen times; then after a pause, other notes and phrases, and so on, pretty well all day long. This manner of singing is irritating, like the staccato song of our throstle, to a listener who wants a continuous stream of song; but it becomes exceedingly interesting when one discovers that the bird is thinking very much about his own music, if one can use such an expression about a bird; that he is all the time experimenting, trying to get a new phrase, a new combination of the notes he knows and new notes. Also, that when sitting on his bush and uttering these careless chance sounds, he is at the same time, intently listening to the others, all engaged in the same way, singing and listening. You will see them all about the place, each bird sitting motionless, like a grey and white image of a bird, on the summit of his own bush. For although he is not gregarious, as a rule a number of pairs live near each other and form a sort of loose community. The bond that unites them is their music, for not only do they sit within hearing distance but they are perpetually mimicking each other. One may say that they are accomplished mimics, but prefer mimicking their own to other species. But they only imitate the notes that take their fancy, so to speak. This, occasionally one strikes out a phrase, a new expression, which appears to please him, and after a few moments he repeats it again, then again, and so on and on, and if you remain an hour within hearing he will perhaps still be repeating it at short intervals. Now if by chance there is something in the new phrase which pleases the listeners too, you will note that they instantly suspend their own singing and for some little time they do nothing but listen. By and by the new note of phrase will be exactly reproduced from a bird on another bush; and he too will begin repeating it at short intervals. Then a second one will get it, then a third, and eventually all the birds in that thicket will have it. The constant repeating of the new note may then go on for hours, and it may last longer. You may return to the spot on the second day and sit for an hour or longer listening and still hear that same note constantly repeated until you are sick and tired of it, or it may even get on your nerves. I remember that on one occasion I avoided a certain thicket, one of my favourite daily haunts, for three whole days not to hear that everlasting sound; then I returned and to my great relief the birds were all at their old game of composing, and not one uttered—perhaps he didn't dare—the too hackneyed phrase."

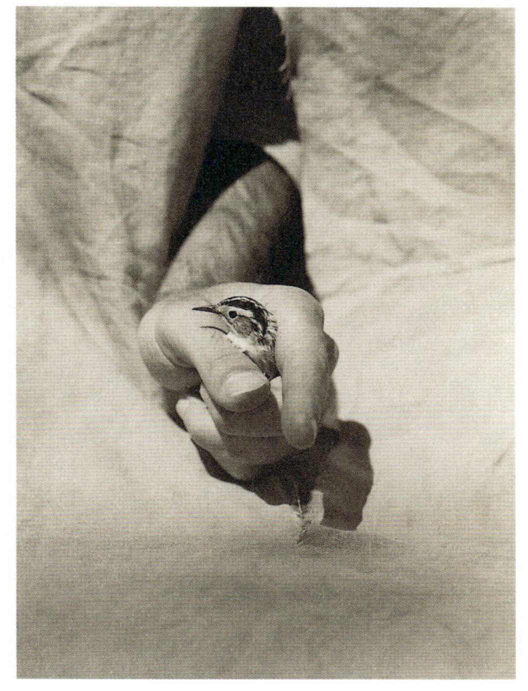

I find Hudson's expression of personal irritation with the mocking-birds very pleasing; I think this is because there is something distantly anthropomorphic about his description of the thought-processes and artistic endeavors of the birds, and I am worried and embarrassed by modern anthropomorphism. (The shameless human-centredness of the mediaeval vision is different.) But Hudson's frank irritation with the birdsong makes him paradoxically at once distant from, and genuinely part of the whole thing that is going on, birds listening to each other and Hudson listening to them, all natural processes. Here, by contrast is a businesslike list of birds, which could stand in for many such lists, made by James Edward, second Earl of Malmesbury.

Killed with my own gun in 40 seasons—ending 1840:—

Black game	81
Partridges	10,744
Quails	50
Landrails	95
Pheasants	6,320
Woodcocks	1,080
Snipes	4,694
Wild swans	3
Wild geese	8
Other wild fowl	2,768
Bitterns	10
Golden plover	6
Hares	5,181
Rabbits	7,414
Grand total	38,454 head

I may average the hours in each day that I was out at full four, one day with another—probably more—which gives me 14,480 hours out in the 40 seasons. Taking the distances walked, on an average allowance for stoppages, and being a very fast walker, at 2 1/2 miles per hour I shall have walked in these 40 seasons full 36,200 miles; very nearly once and ahalf of the circumference of the Globe.

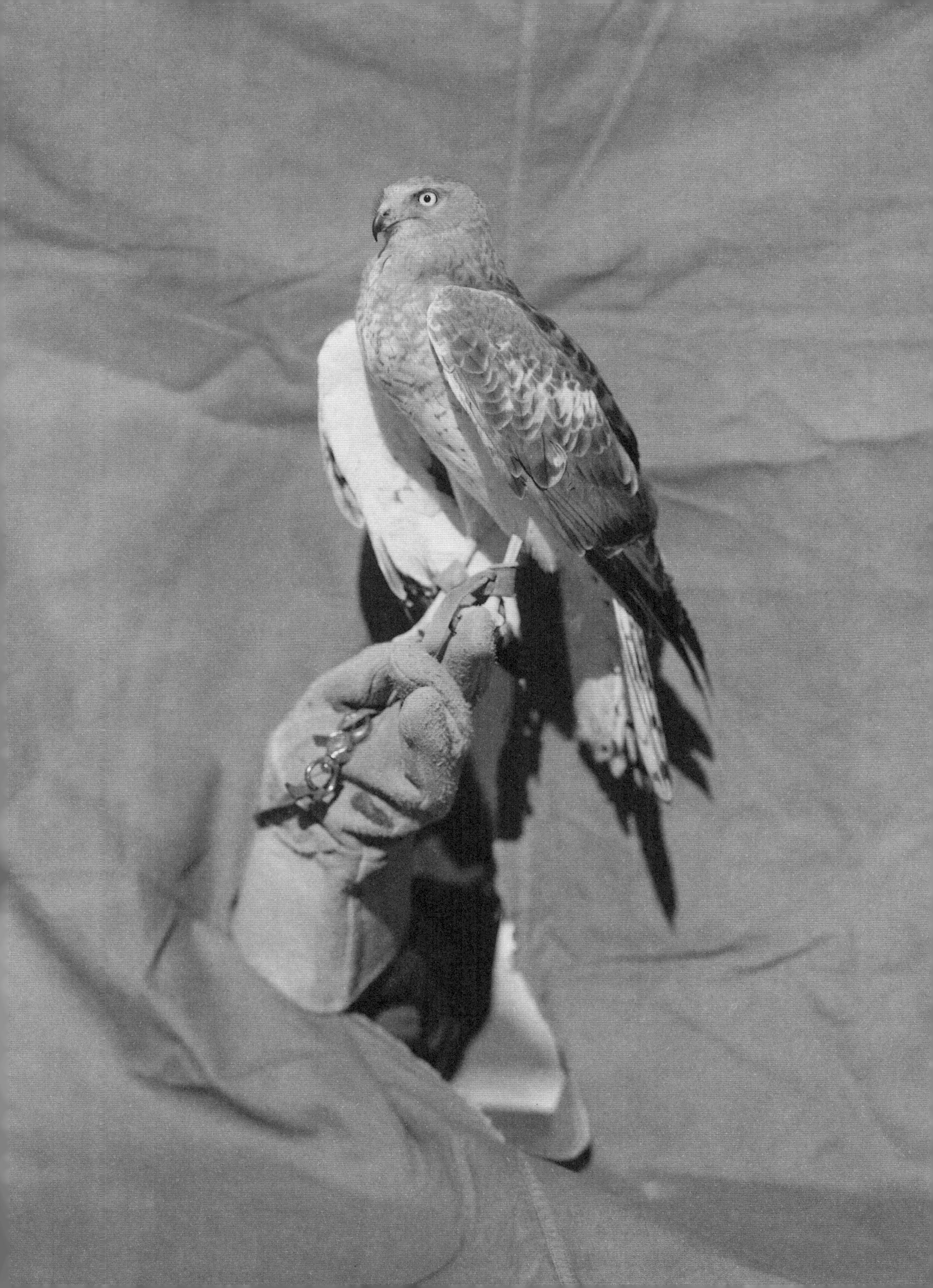

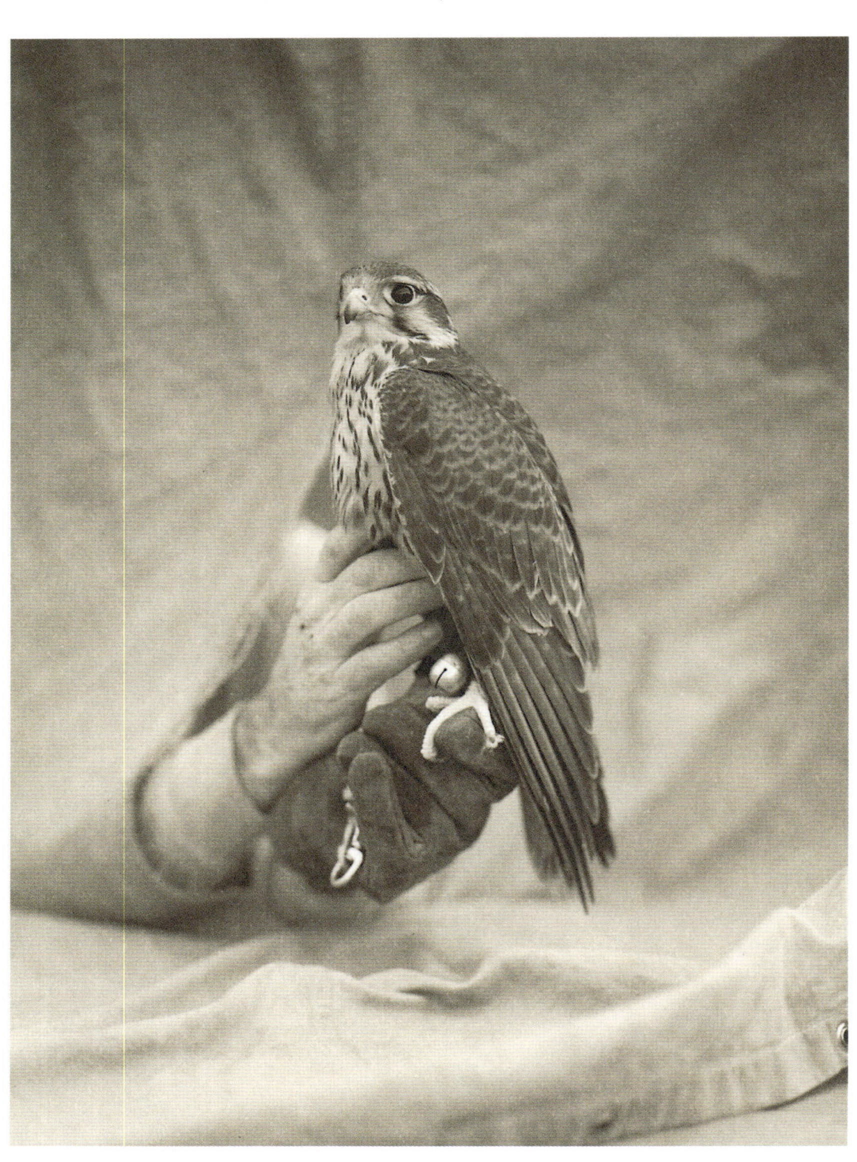

HARRIS HAWK

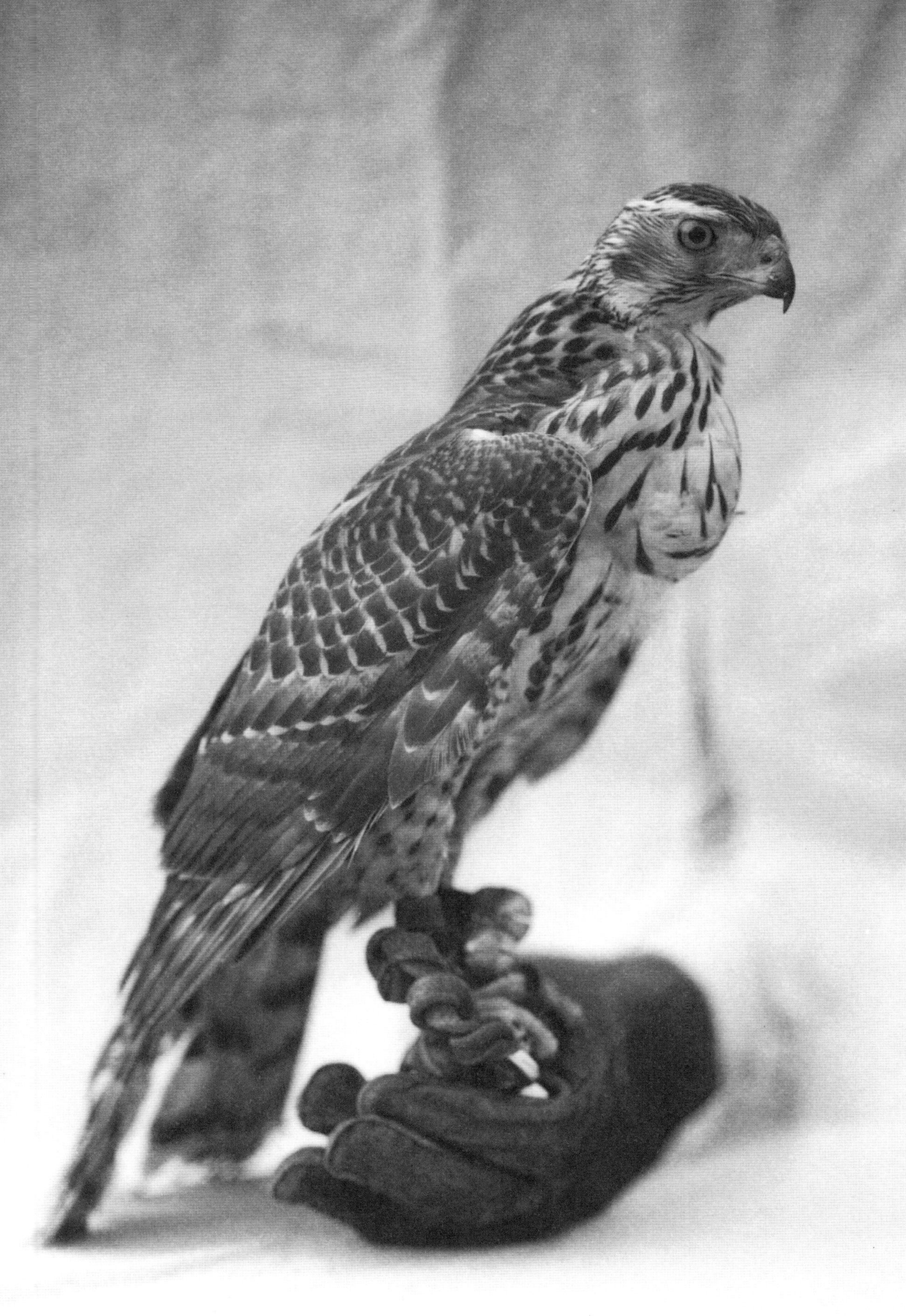

SWAINSON'S HAWK

The slaughter of birds in the great shooting parties of the Edwardian upper classes in Britain has been seen as a precursor of the slaughter of the young men in the First World War—more efficient weapons producing mass death. Twentieth century thoughts about birds are couloured by our anxiety about what we are doing to them, and to the earth—the anxiety is moving, even if the acts of destruction are frightening. Rachel Carson's *Silent Spring* in 1962 has a quotation from Keats as its epigraph: "the sedge is wither'd from the lake / And no birds sing." She gives a terrifying list of birds killed by pesticides in the spring of 1961.

Then came the spring of 1961, when tens of thousands of birds were found littering the country-side, dead or dying in agony. The story from one estate alone reveals the nature of the tragedy... From the royal estate at Sandring-ham in Norfolk the list of dead birds included pheasants, red-legged partridges, partridges, woodpigeons, and stock doves, greenfinches, chaffinches, black-birds, song thrushes, skylarks, moorhens, bramblings, tree sparrows, house sparrows, jays, yellow-hammers, hedge sparrows, carrion crows, hooded crows, gold-finches, and sparrowhawks. Over 142 bodies were collected in 11 1/2 hours of special survey counts, and hundreds more over a period of weeks. Among these birds were some, such as the bramblings, which are specially protected by law, yet all went down before the indiscriminate scythe of toxic chemicals.

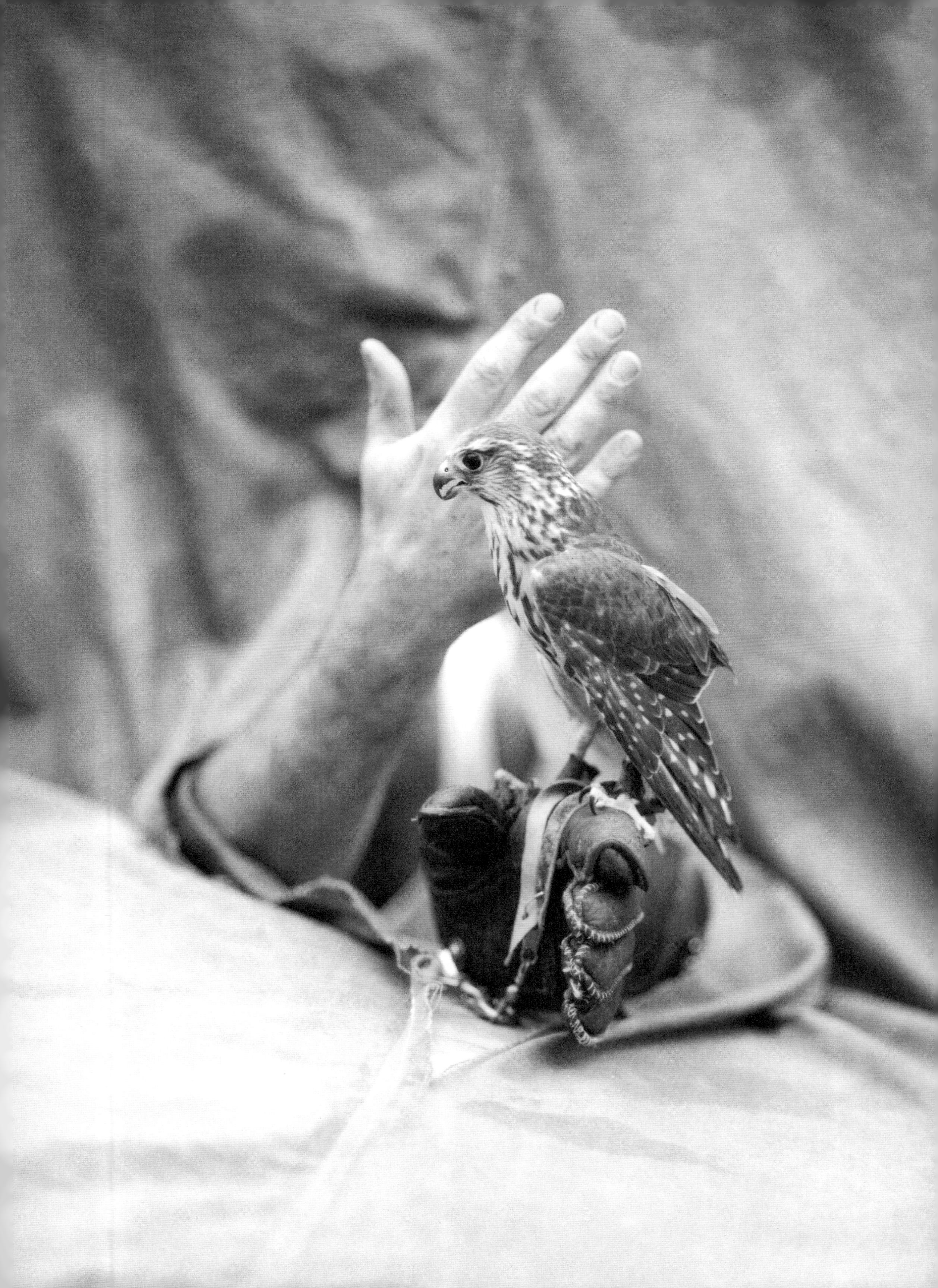

Carson described an assault by spray-plane and parathion in southern Indiana in 1959, on a group of blackbirds that were feeding in the cornfields. She claims that the problem could have been solved by changing the variety of corn, but that in the event the spraying killed 65,000 red-winged blackbirds and starlings, without taking any account of other wildlife. Carson asks, with a rhetoric that has been partly persuasive since her time

Who has made the decision that sets in motion these chains of poisonings, this ever-widening wave of death that spreads out, like ripple when a pebble is dropped into a still pond? Who has placed in one pan of the scale the leaves that might have been eaten by the beetles and in the other the pitiful heaps of many-hued feathers, the lifeless remains of the birds that fell before the unselective bludgeons of insecticidal poison. Who has decided who has the *right* to decide—for the countless legions of people who were not consulted that the supreme value is a world without insects, even though it be also a sterile world ungraced by the curving wing of a bird in flight?

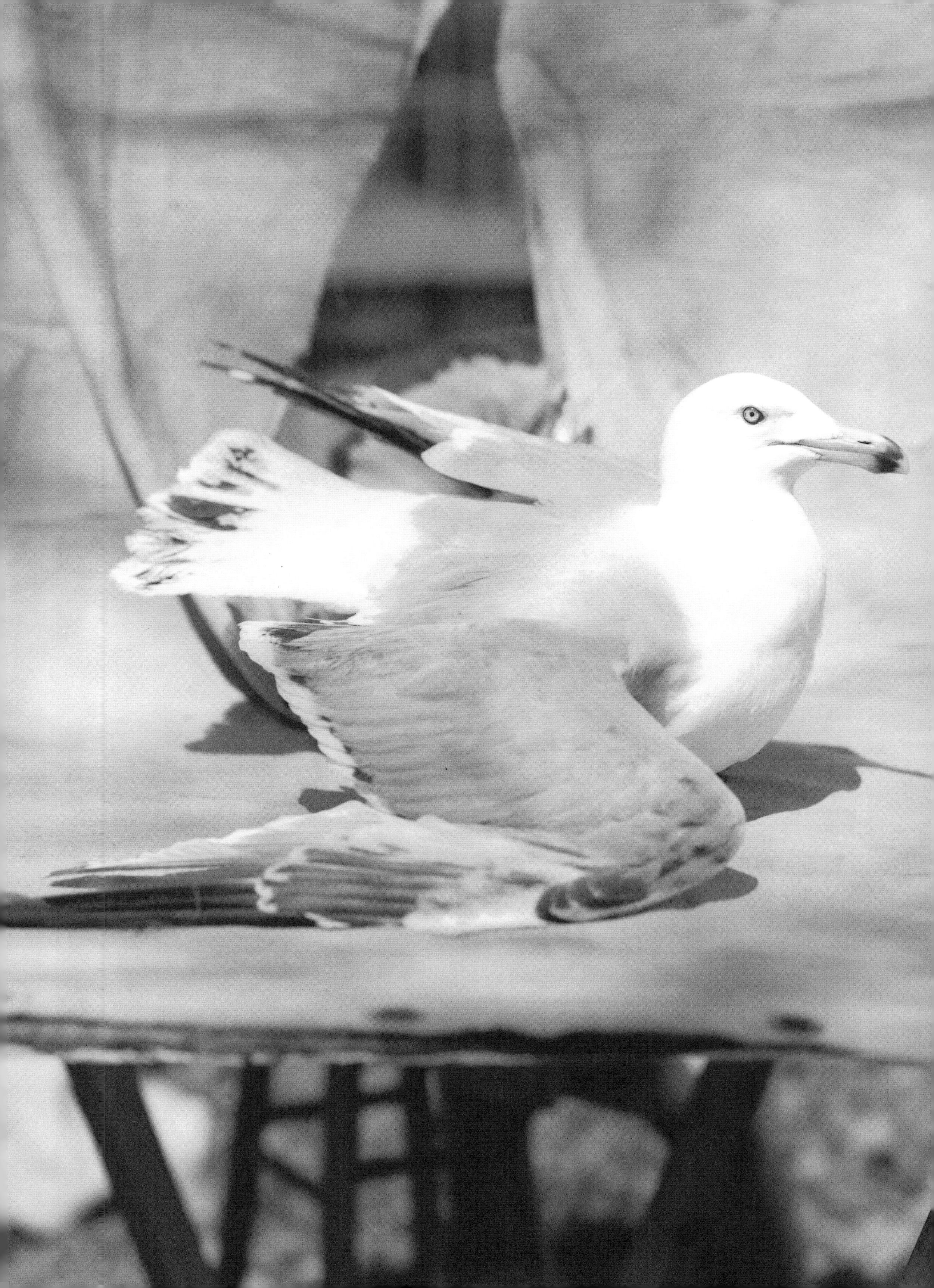

Ours is an age of anxiety about the creatures and our relations with them. One of the best accounts I know of this anxiety is Margaret Visser's meditation, in her bestseller *Much Depends on Dinner*, on the chicken, the bird closest to us, though, as she says, one that has "seldom roused people's affections—they are too scratchy, self-absorbed, un-mammalian, and above all, too edible for that." Visser's chapter on chickens includes information about their uses in classical divination, their relations with the sun-gods of various cultures, fighting cocks and farmyard habits. She has a delightful etymological list:

> *Gallus* is the Roman name for the bird; some have thought that the name refers to France, *Gallia*, which may have been one early introducer of chickens to the Italian peninsula, Greek Sicily being the other. It is much more likely, however, that *gallus* comes from the same root as the word "poultry." This root is the Hindu word *pil*, which becomes *pullus* and *gallus* (Latin) *pollo* (Italian), *poulet* (French) and *pullet* (English). Another widely-used stem for words designating chickens is thought also to originate in India: it is *kuk*, Sanskrit *kukata*, Latin *cucurio*, *kuku*, in many African languages, *Kuchlein* (German), *coq* (French) *kieken* (Dutch) *cock* and *chicken* in English.

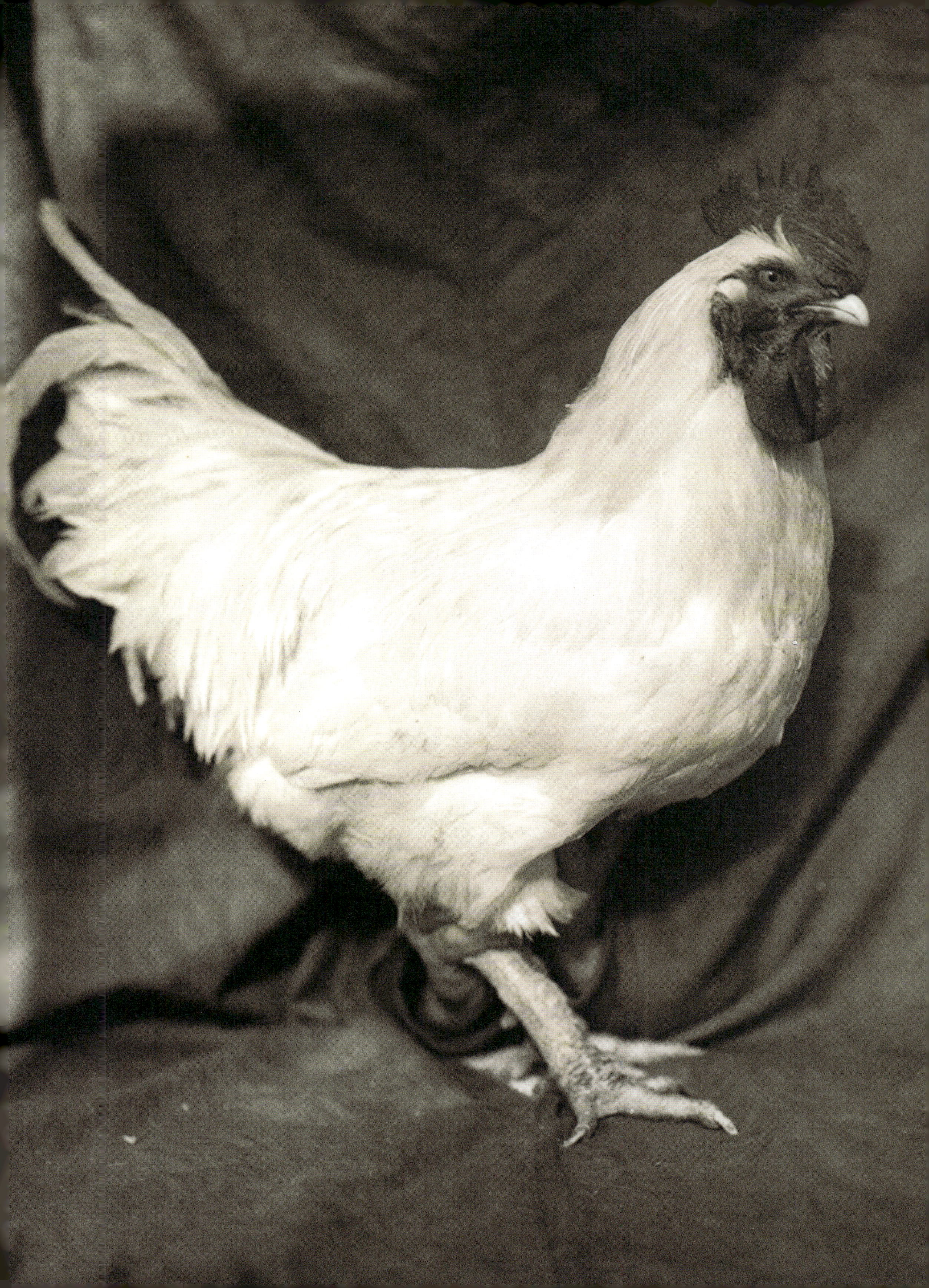

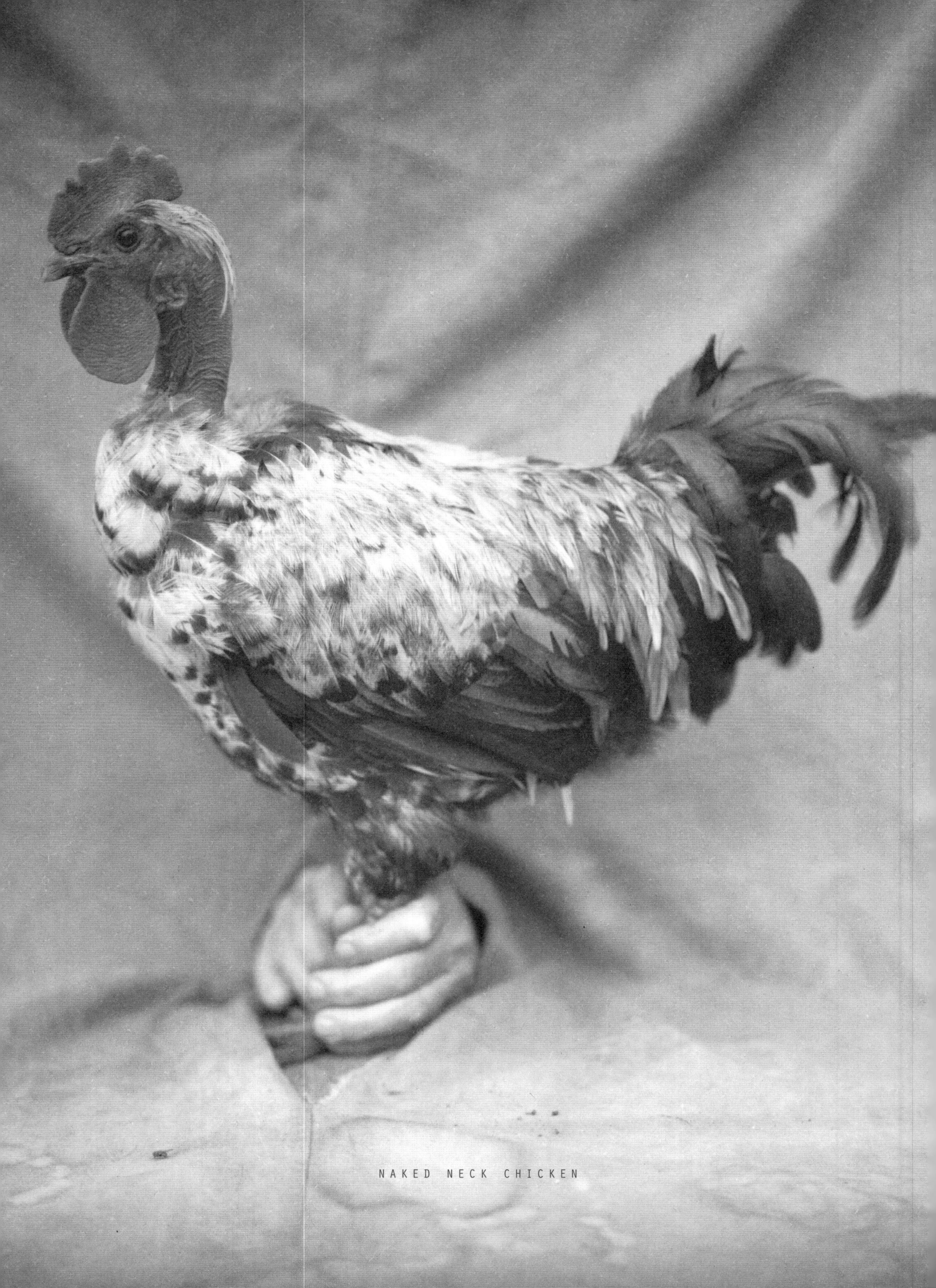

NAKED NECK CHICKEN

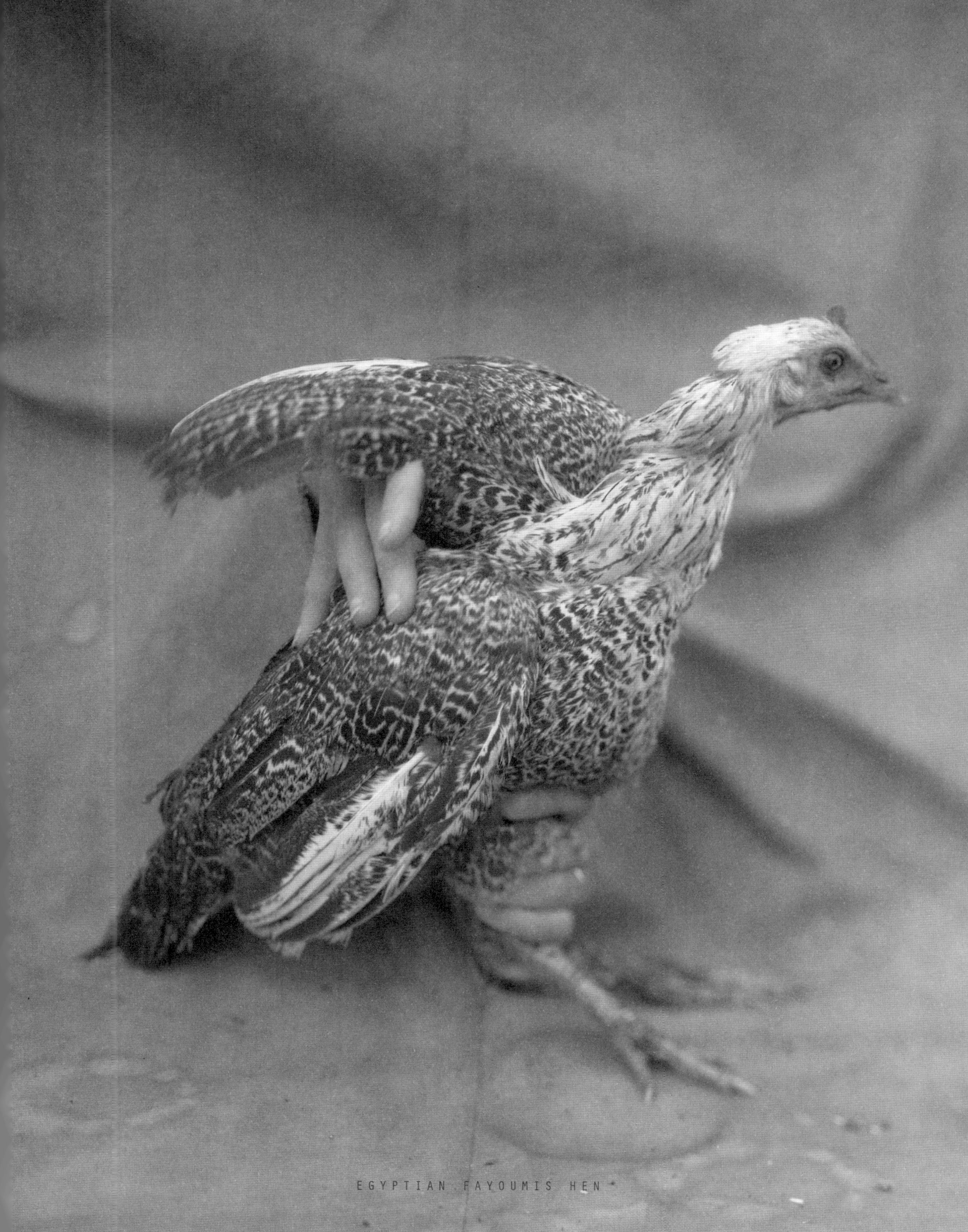

EGYPTIAN FAYOUMIS HEN

But her lists of what is done to this unfortunate bird by modern farming and food industries make chilling and distressing reading. The meat, the "harvested crop" or "product" is so sanitised by the time it reaches the human eaters that many never see anything other than regular packs of "white" meat, with no bird-shape and much less bird-taste than the legs and thighs. My list of lists began with birds in Paradise. Here is the other end, so to speak, the processing of chickens.

The chicken catchers go out from the meat-packing company to bring in the birds for slaughter. They do this at night, since as chicken-raisers have known for thousands of years, drowsy fowl are easier to handle than cackling, flapping, awake ones. The trucks, each bearing several thousand chickens, return to the slaughterhouse with the greatest dispatch, to minimise "shrinkage." This is the trade's name for the loss of weight and the death of some of the chickens, which takes place between collecting and loading fowl and slaughtering them. Factors which cause "shrinkage" are crowded cages, lack of air (chickens need three times as much air as human beings do, yet they are commonly crated for transport as if they needed none) rough handling, struggle and excretion during the change....

When the working day begins at the slaughterhouse the birds are hung upside down by their feet on moving conveyor belts and passed through a vat full of an electrically charged salt solution, where most, though not all, are shocked senseless....

The line moves without stopping to the Kill Room where automatic blades slit throats. The file of bodies passes into the Bleed Tunnel, where most of the blood is vacuum-sucked out of the birds in fifty seconds or less.... An insufficiently-bled fowl will have a blotchy appearance which is unacceptable to shoppers. Blood is not part of the chicken-meat myth.

Next the procession moves on to the Scalding Tank, where hot water loosens the feathers. Plucking is done mechanically. Rubber fingers protrude from the sides of a tunnel through which the chickens travel.... The chickens are singed to remove any remaining body hair; their heads are jerked away and their feet chopped off, automatically; and polyphosphates are injected to prolong shelf-life....

Government inspectors pass and grade each "finished" bird and finally the chickens are packaged and frozen, or taken in trucks to supermarkets to be sold "fresh."... The chickens which have not made the grade—because of skin bruises, tears or blisters, broken bones, or bluish flesh owing to insufficient fat beneath the skin—are turned over for use in pet food, canned chicken soup and bouillon cubes, or are emulsified in such products as frankfurters, bologna, and summer sausage. The feet are exported in large numbers to the Orient, where chicken feet are considered delicious, not sinister, or too reminiscent of a living creature, as they are for many of us. Feathers are processed and used in chicken feed mixes.

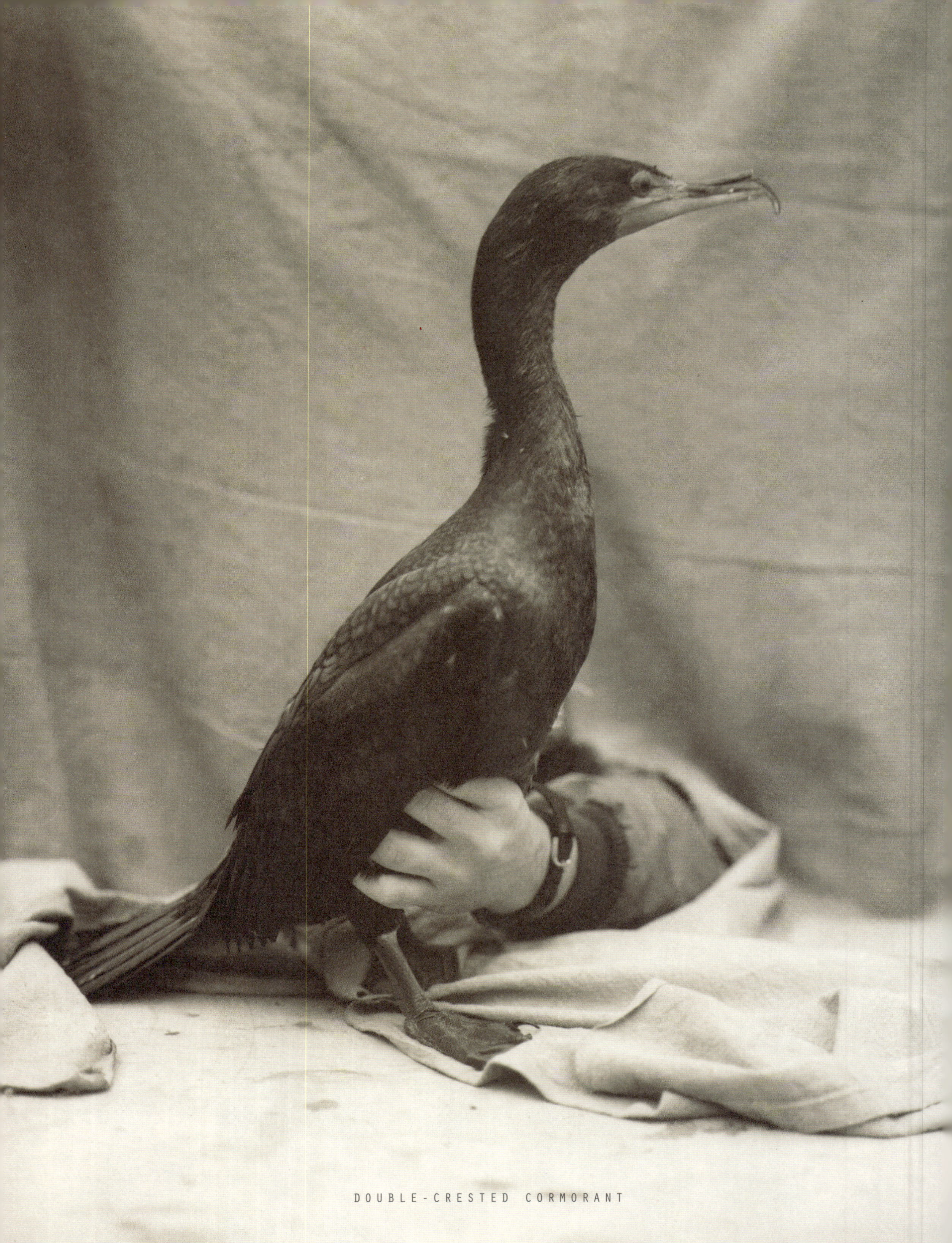

DOUBLE-CRESTED CORMORANT

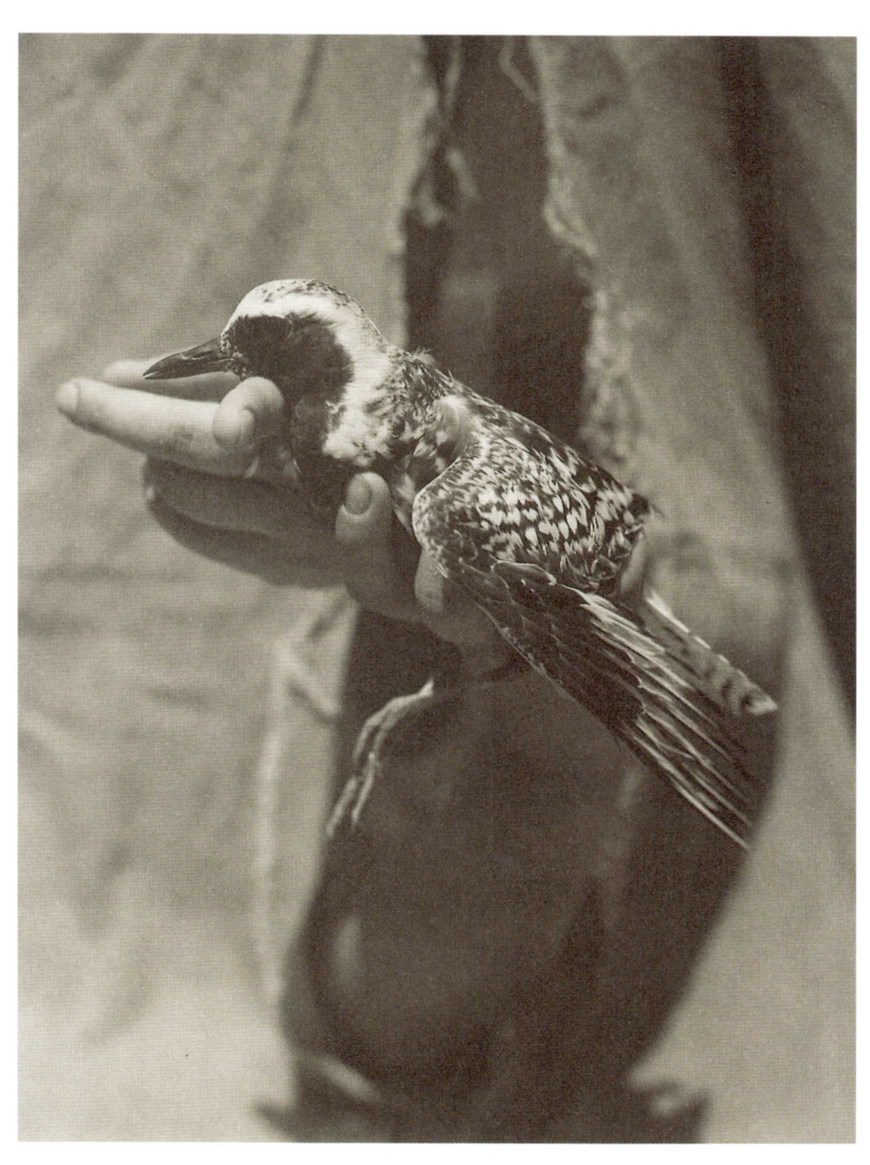

BLACK-BELLIED PLOVER

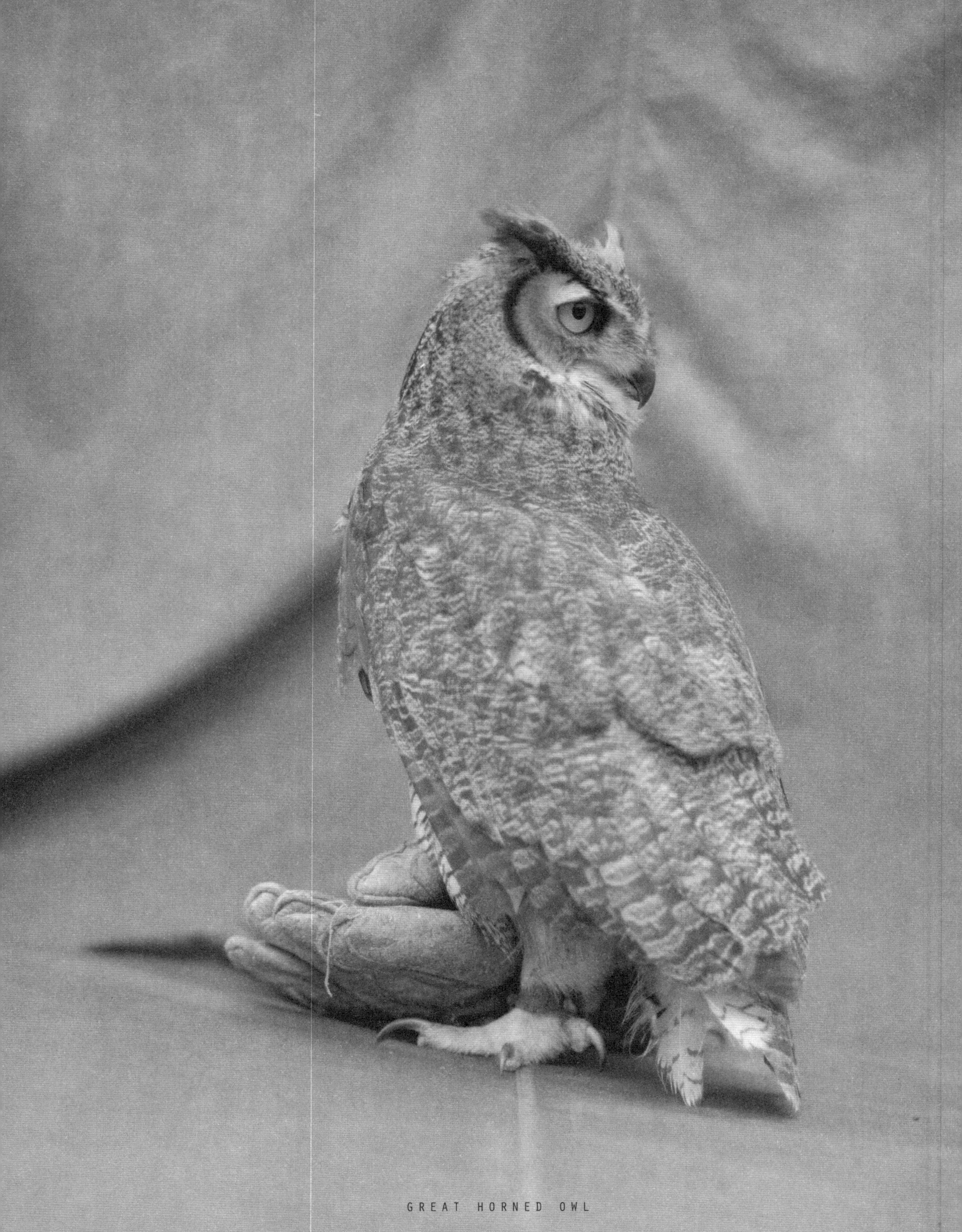

GREAT HORNED OWL

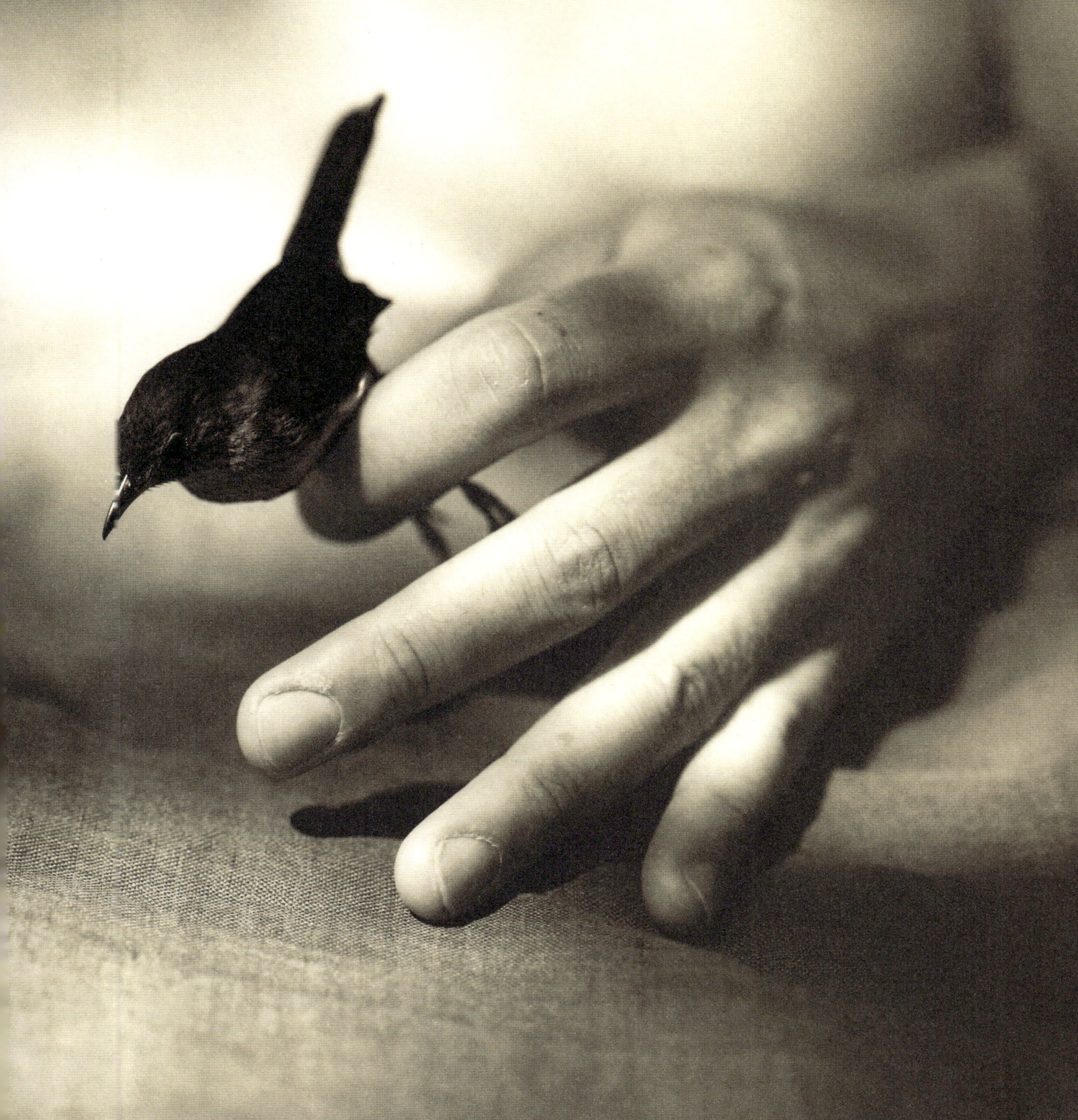

HOUSE WREN

I don't want to end on human inhumanity to birds. Whilst I was in Filey, on the North Yorkshire Coast recently, on a cold January day, I found in a small café on a bleak cliff-top the *Filey Brigg Bird Report* for 1944. The Brigg is a long rocky peninsula that stretches out from the cliffs into the North Sea, and the birdwatchers or twitchers clearly keep a year-long vigil on cliffs and in fields, recording migrants and yearly fluctuations in populations. The Oxford English Dictionary defines a "twitcher" as a "birdwatcher whose main object is to catch sightings of rare birds" and suggests, *inter alia*, that the word derives from a distinction between birdwatchers and serious ornithologists, in that the twitchers only want to tick rare birds off on a list—twitch being related to a tick. A kinder definition is that they are those who begin to "twitch" with excitement when "south-east winds blow and the headlands begin to bristle with Pied Flycatchers and Redstarts." I travel with a taxi-driver whose life has been transfigured by twitching—he spends his holidays in the Costa Rican rainforest, or travelling across the Indian plains on elephant-back armed with binoculars and camera, observing birds. The *Filey Brigg Bird Report* contains wonderful lists of birds seen, too long to reproduce—I can quote figures. Between 1977, 1983–93, and 1994, the watchers ringed 13,155 birds from 102 species, whose names read like a long Anglo-Saxon poem, or a Linnaean taxonomy, beginning:— Storm Petrel Sparrowhawk Kestrel Water Rail Grey Plover Lapwing Knot Purple Sandpiper Dunlin, and ending Arctic Redpoll Crossbill Common Rosefinch Bullfinch Yellowhammer Rustic Bunting Little Bunting Reed Bunting. The monthly journal of the birdwatchers is a record of humans and birds meeting in all sorts of weathers, all sorts of movements of air and wind and sea. I will quote the entry for October 1994.

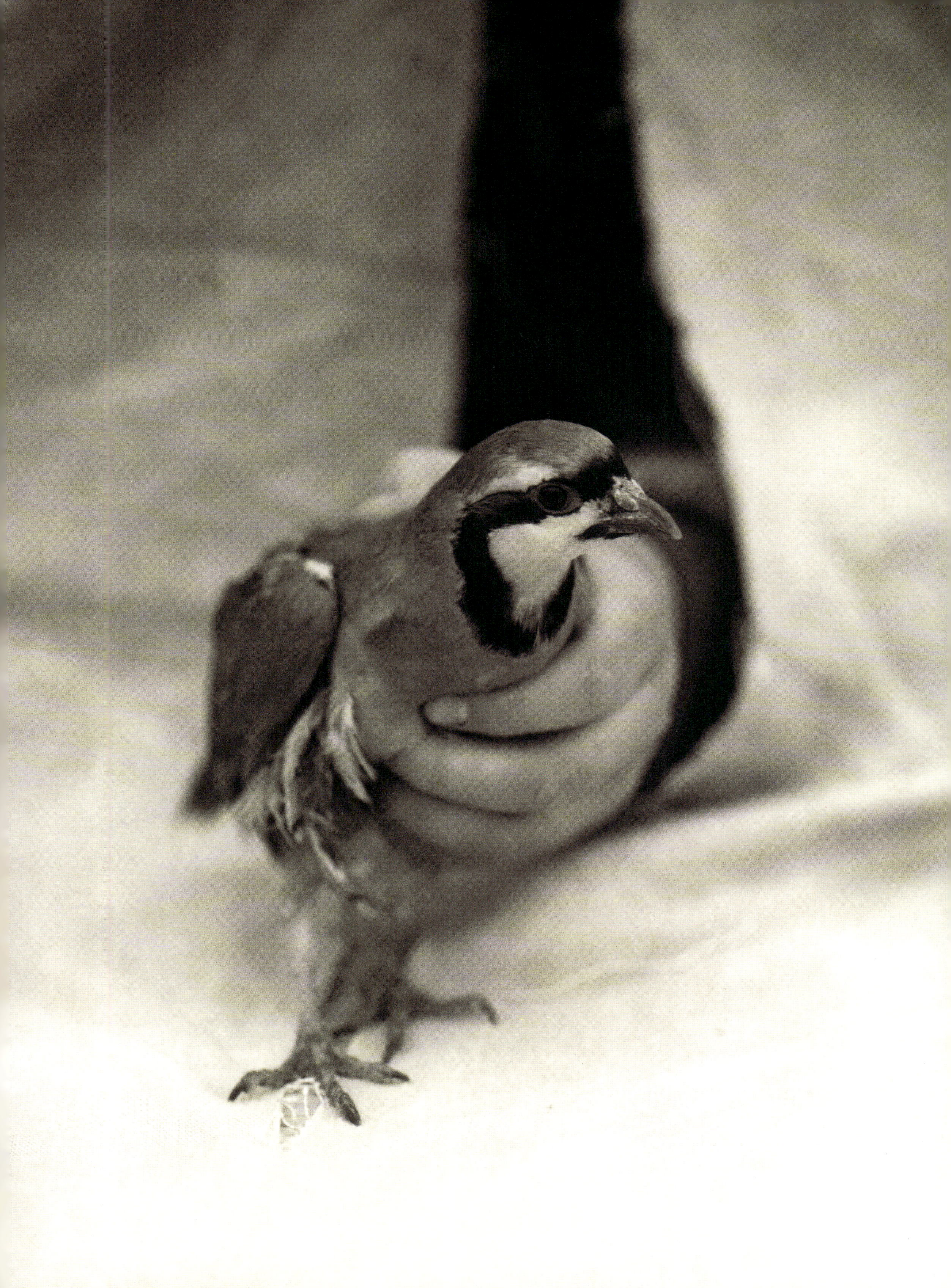

In fact the month began quietly, two Yellow-Browed Warblers on 2nd being the result of some rather indifferent weather. Strong northerlies on 3rd livened things up, particularly at sea, where 11 Long-tailed Skuas, 37 Pomarine Skuas and a Sabine's Gull were forced to move past the Brigg. Next day another Long-tailed Skua went north and a first winter Glaucous Gull flew south. The 5th saw a Slavonian Grebe flying north, while single Yellow-browed and Barred Warblers were found at the dams. Light south-westerlies put a damper on the next few days, but as the winds became more southerly on 9th, Filey suddenly changed...into Fair Isle! On that fateful day, an elusive pipit in the totem pole field gradually revealed itself to be a Pechora Pipit, the first twitchable mainland record if you could drive fast enough. Meanwhile a Richard's Pipit flew north over Primrose Valley. Next day, through their tears, late arrivers searching for the now departed Pechora stumbled on a Lanceolated Warbler on Carr Naze. No one could believe it and many tried not to, until its identity was proved in the hands of the ringers. By now the wind was south-easterly and on 11th there were three Yellow-browed Warblers and a Jay. Perhaps it was Filey after all! A few quiet days followed until a brief return to north-easterlies on 16th resulted in a long-tailed Skua circling over the top fields and an all-too-brief Arctic Redpoll in the top scrub. Next day a Hooded Crow was seen and on 18th another Yellow-browed Warbler. By 20th the wind had been south-easterly for several days. This produced a Firecrest and two Common Buzzards. The 21st saw the arrival of a Richard's Pipit, and probably, a Barred Warbler, though the latter was only confirmed on 23rd by which time the wind was south-westerly. Such conditions sometimes produce large raptors, and this year was to be particularly fruitful; two Rough-legged Buzzards and two Common Buzzards occurred on 23rd, two Hen Harriers on 24th, another Hen Harrier the next day, and by 26th there were four Common Buzzards in the area. Passerines discovered at the same time included a Shore Lark on 24th and another Yellow-breasted Warbler on 25th and a total of 514 Pink-footed Geese flew south from 26th to 28th. The Hooded Crow was still around on 29th and a Crossbill was found on 30th.

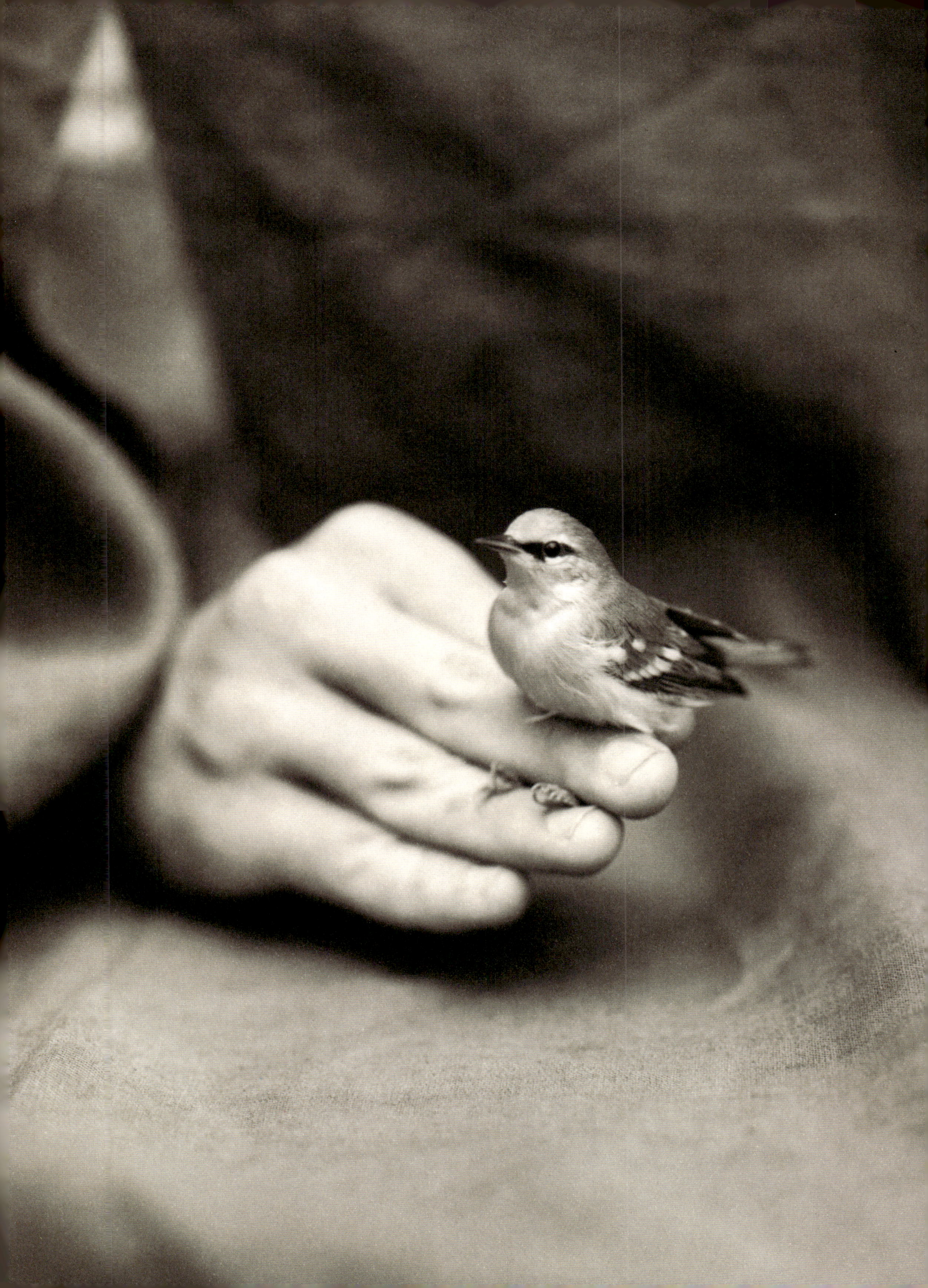

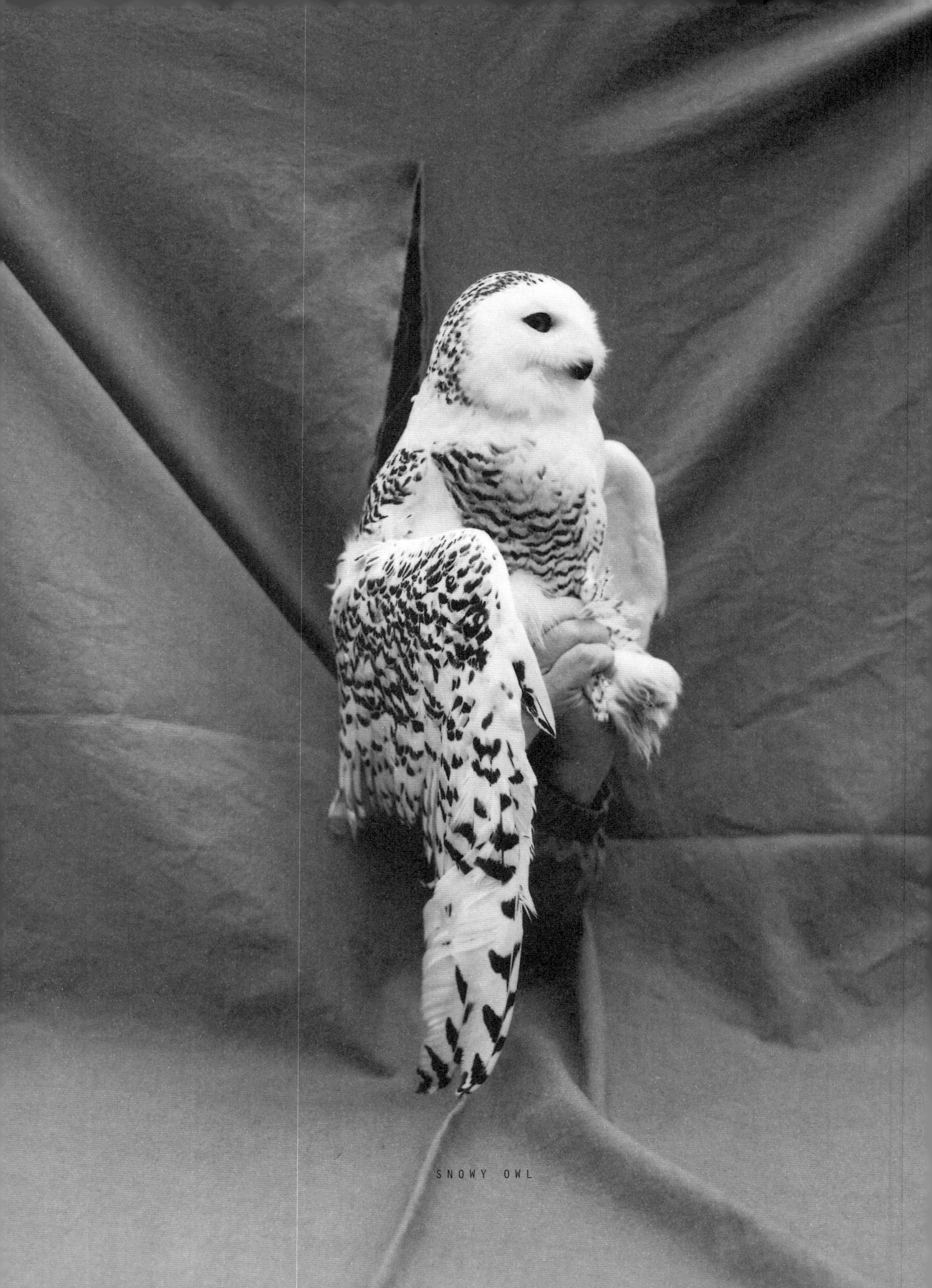

SNOWY OWL

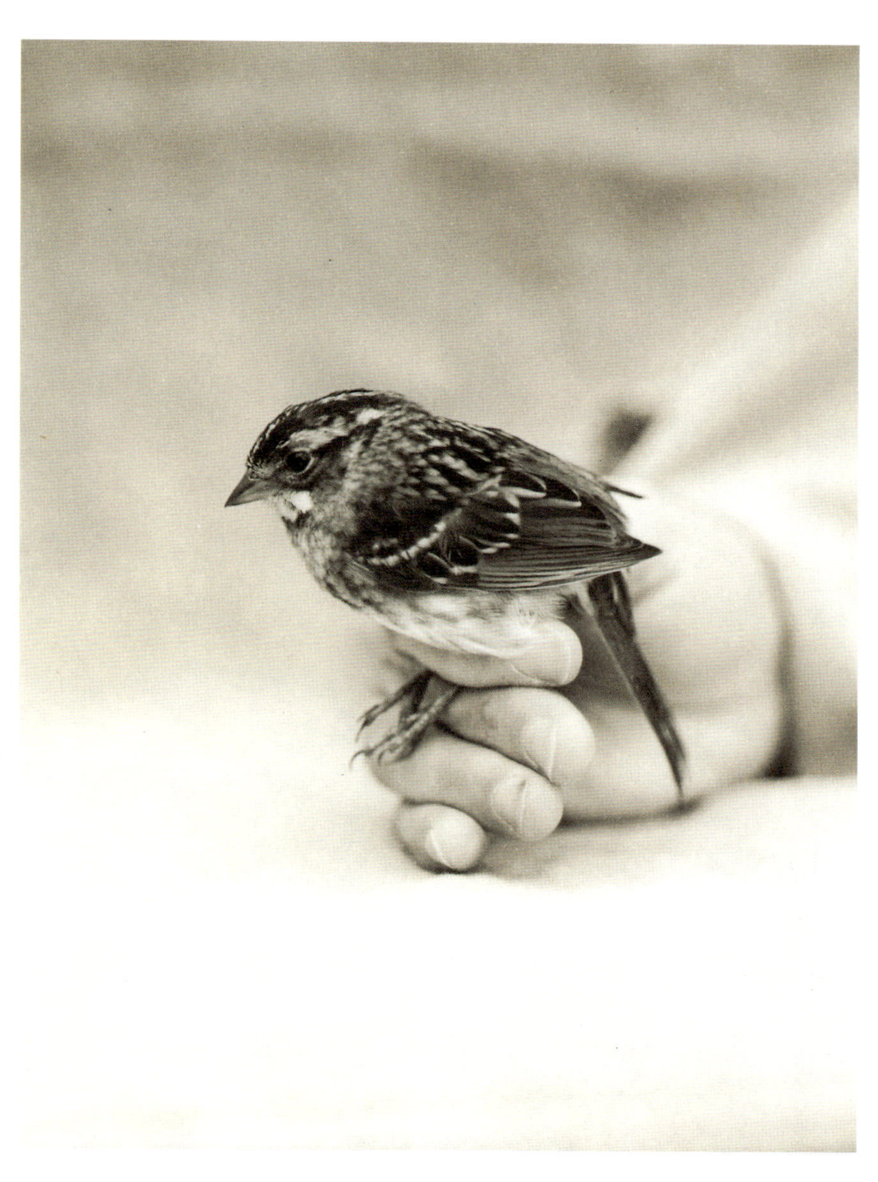

WHITE-THROATED SPARROW

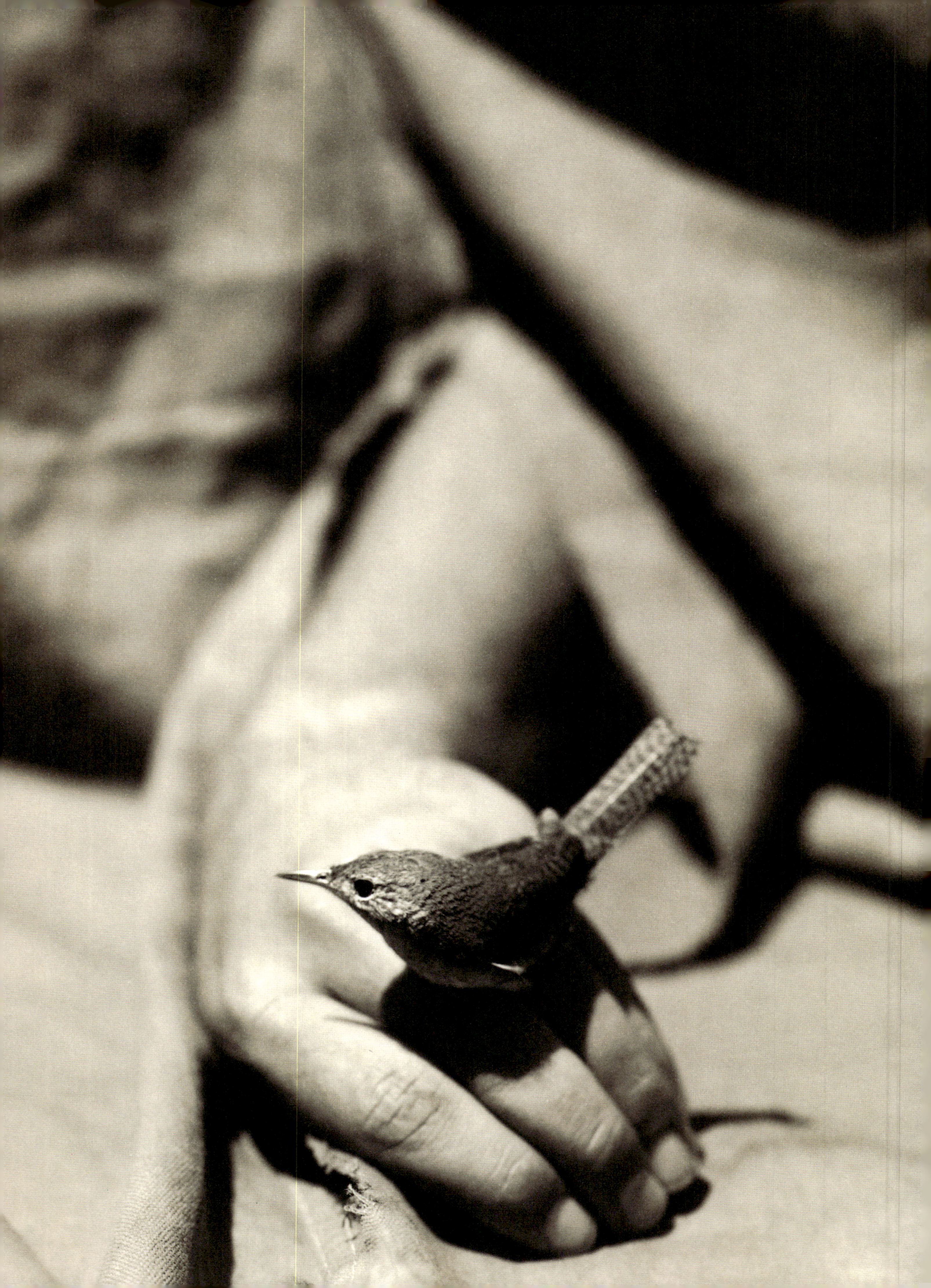

This is passionate writing by a human to whom the winds are interesting and studied for the birds they might bring. The account of the discovery and identification of the Pechora Pipit is dramatic, comic, and a fitting place to end my list of lists.... The report comes from Craig Thomas, who saw the pipit "drop into thick ground vegetation" in the totem pole field at Carr Naze. He flushed the bird once or twice and thought it might be a Red-throated Pipit.

After waiting a further ten minutes without another view I called Pete Dunn over on the CB, and before other FBOG members arrived we were able to re-locate the pipit after a frustrating ten minute wait. Over the next 1½ hours several observers were treated to flight views, with just a couple managing brief views on the ground. Although Pechora Pipit was mentioned, all those present seemed happy with the Identification as Red-throated Pipit.

By mid-morning the sun had burned through the mist and greater numbers of birders present were able to pin down the elusive bird in improved light. As it dried out the "Dulux" white tramlines and double wing bars literally shone, and with some observers seeing a primary projection, the bird was identified as a Pechora Pipit. In order to clear up any potential discrepancies, the pipit was trapped and the in-hand identification confirmed the rarer species. After processing it was released back into the totem pole field, where it gave sporadic views for the rest of the day.

With only a handful of accepted mainland records, and constituting the first twitchable mainland record, the Pechora Pipit attracted a maximum of 900 birders during the afternoon.
As a result of its sporadic appearances the crowds often built up to over 400 individuals, often completely encircling the bird in its favourite feeding areas. Such an arrangement allowed people at opposite sides of the circle to view the pipit. No doubt such crowd behaviour must have looked very strange to walkers along the cliff top!

There is something mysterious as well as absurd in this spectacle of 900 humans engaged in viewing one small bird. It could be an emblem of the modern world, where we are the species that has crowded out all others. But it is not that—it is also an image of human beings fiercely involved in the natural world, full of pure, disinterested curiosity, making lists of names out of pride in local recording and human knowledge.

My list of lists has complicated my own ideas of the relations between birds and men, and my ideas of what birds are—taxonomically, poetically, anatomically, anthropomorphically, etymologically, mythologically, commercially. Victor Schrager's photographs add another dimension to the mystery of human-bird relations. We feel ambivalent about the relation of the series of hands to the series of birds. We look at the birds, the similarities and the differences, we categorize and catalogue, we form our own emotional and metaphorical responses to them. They look out of the page with the eyes that do, and don't, resemble our own. We love them, we are curious about them, we tell ourselves tales, magical and scientific, anthropomorphic and ecological about them. My list of lists has many tones of voice and points of view. It is, as I said at the beginning, a *human* undertaking; language is what differentiates humans from other creatures. We describe the birds, but we don't know or possess them. It is true that the eye of the camera is a man-made eye, and that the artist chooses what we shall see of the birds. What he records is beautiful and complex. He shows us the birds as he sees them, but he doesn't know or possess them either. The photographs convey to me, in their serial similarity and difference, with an immediacy that language can never achieve,

the mystery of the otherness of birds.

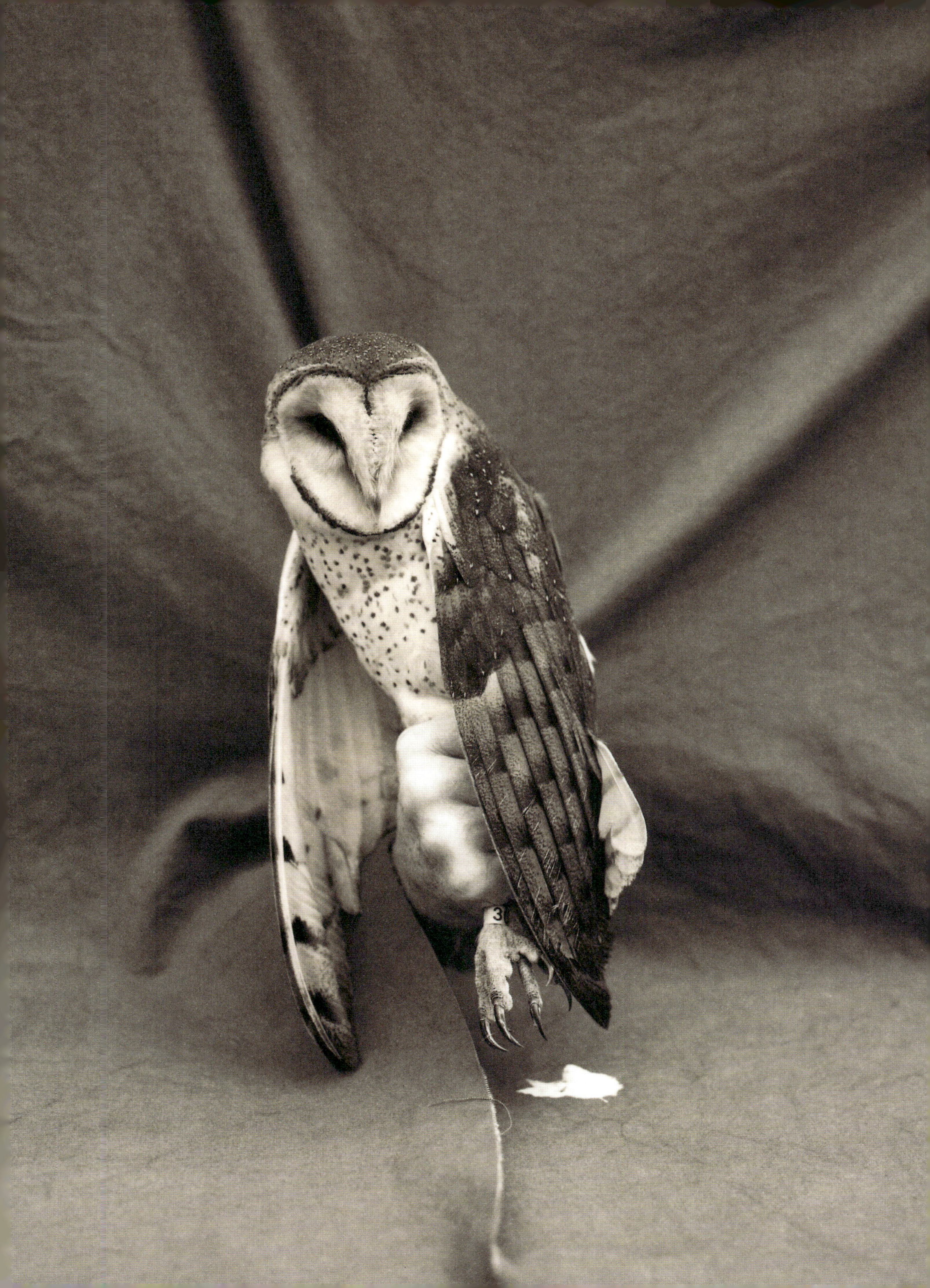

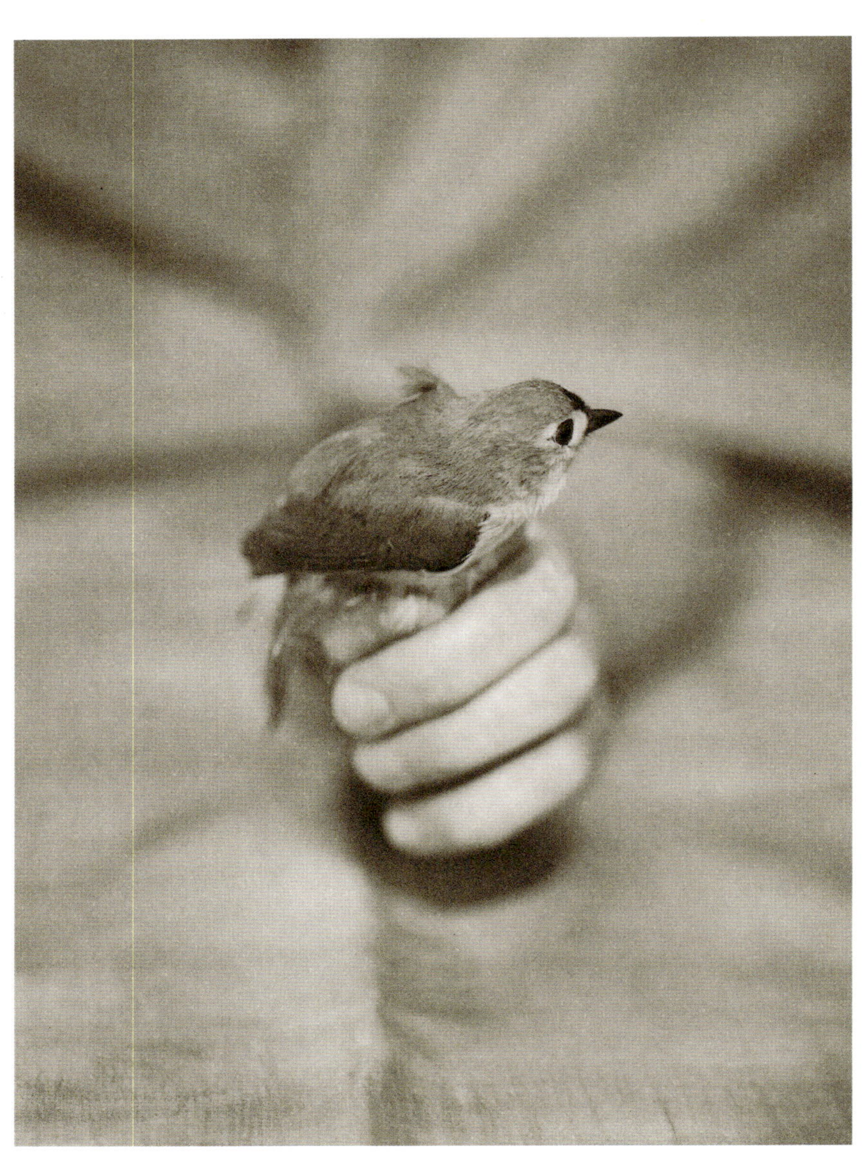

TUFTED TITMOUSE

PLATES

6. white rock chicken

9. hermit thrush

10. grackle

11. barred owl

14. peregrine falcon

17. black-capped chickadees

18. bluebird

20. zebra finch

21. brown pelican

22. carolina wren

23. screech owl

24. snowy owl

25. short-eared owl

26. bronze turkey

27. ovenbird

28. turkey vulture

29. dark-eyed junco

30. guinea cock

31. blue jay

32. house sparrows

33. house finch

34. downy woodpecker

35. screech owls

39. snowy egret

41. buff cochin chicken

42. catbird

43. green-backed heron

44. robin

47. marbled godwit

49. golden eagle

50. black rosecomb chicken

51. yellow-breasted chat

53. cardinal

55. kestrel

58. blue-winged warbler
canada warbler
myrtle warbler
chestnut-sided warbler

59. black & white warblers

61. purple martin

64. least tern

65. moorhen

66. great grey owl

67. saw-whet owl

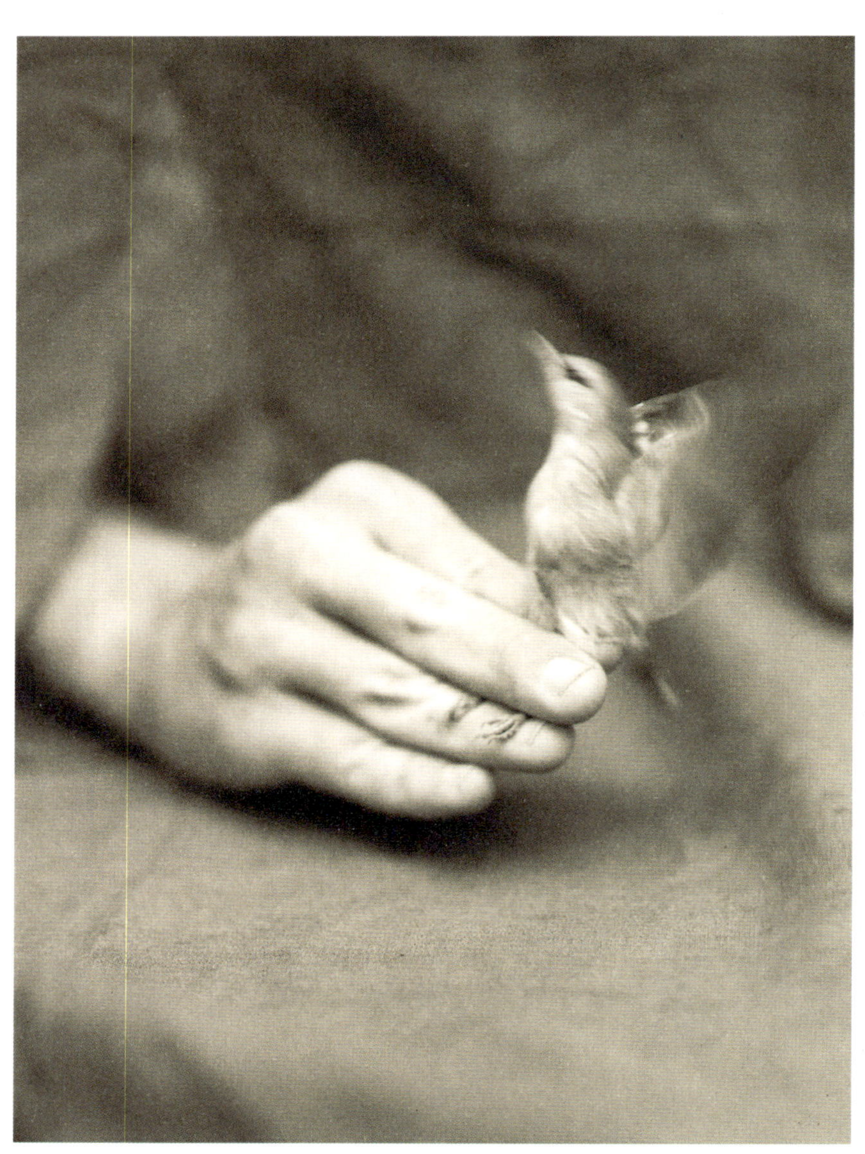

WARBLER

68. ring-necked pheasant

69. ring-necked pheasant

70. silver sebright chicken

71. bearded golden polish bantam chicken

72. house wren nestlings

73. burrowing owl

74. passenger pigeon (extinct)

75. hybrid pigeon

76. hybrid pigeon

77. hybrid pigeon

79. hybrid pigeon

80. ruby-throated hummingbird

81. crow

82. cedar waxwing

83. black-capped chickadee

84. tri-colored heron

85. laughing gull

86. black rosecomb chicken

87. tufted titmouse

88. buff cochin chicken

89. old english silver duckwing game bantam chicken

91. magnolia warbler

93. black & white warbler

95. harrier

96. harris hawk

97. swainson's hawk

99. merlin

101. herring gull

103. white orpington chicken

104. naked neck chicken

105. egyptian fayoumis hen

108. double-crested cormorant

109. black-bellied plover

110. great horned owl

111. house wren

113. chukar partridge

115. brewster's warbler

116. snowy owl

117. white-throated sparrow

118. house wren

121. barn owl

122. tufted titmouse

124. warbler

I would like to express my appreciation to the following individuals and institutions for their assistance with this work:

Michelle Adams; Tom Alworth, Isabella Scheiber, and the Edward Niles Huyck Preserve and Biological Field Station, Rensselaerville, New York; Mike Brust, Sarah Karpanty, Patricia Pelkowski, Mary Richards, and the Theodore Roosevelt Wildlife Sanctuary, Oyster Bay, New York; Ted Bryan; Lee Buttala; Nicholas Callaway; Dr. John Carpenter; Virginia Carter; Wendy Cromer; Orrin Devinsky; Peter Douglas; James Dunlinson; Mari Faucher; Dan Froelich and the Institute for Bird Populations, Point Reyes Station, California; the Geurtze family; Teddy Grill; the John Simon Guggenheim Foundation; Ann Giordano; Agnethe Glatved; Amy Goldberger; Belinda Haas; Philip Haas; Sarah Hasted; Ralph Heath and the Suncoast Seabird Sanctuary, Indian Shores, Florida; Mark Holborn; Jenni Holder; Edwynn Houk; Sharon Curtis Kalaji; Mame Kennedy; Georgia Liebman; the Mabey family; Peter MacGill; Albert Miller; Ellie Miller; Hannah Milman; Delphine Posson; Sarah Buffum Prud'homme; Margaret Roach; Sally Ruppert and Volunteers for Wildlife, Caumsett State Park, Lloyd's Neck, New York; Dr. Len Soucy and the Raptor Trust, Millington, New Jersey; Ray Starr III; David Steadman; Luisa Stevenson; Martha Stewart; Gael Towey; Barbara de Wilde; Wing Haven Garden, Charlotte, North Carolina; Karen Wise; Jonathan Wood and the Raptor Project, Roxbury, New York; Doug Wolske, Andrea Birnbaum, Michael Gerbino, B. Martin Pedersen and GRAPHIS, New York City; Wing Haven Garden, Charlotte, North Carolina.

My special thanks to Stephen Doyle for his encouragement, insight, and support during all phases of this project, and for his brilliant design of this book. He has, with associate Rosemarie Turk at Doyle Partners, given life to a particularly complex body of words and pictures.

—VICTOR SCHRAGER

I should like to thank the following for their contributions to my text:

Claus Bech, who led me to the quotations from St. Francis; Amy Goldberger, for her help with permissions; the London Library, whose idiosyncratic cataloguing system was even more helpful than usual; Gill Marsden, for her help in preparing the manuscript; and John Saumarez Smith, who found me a copy of T.H. White.

— A.S. BYATT

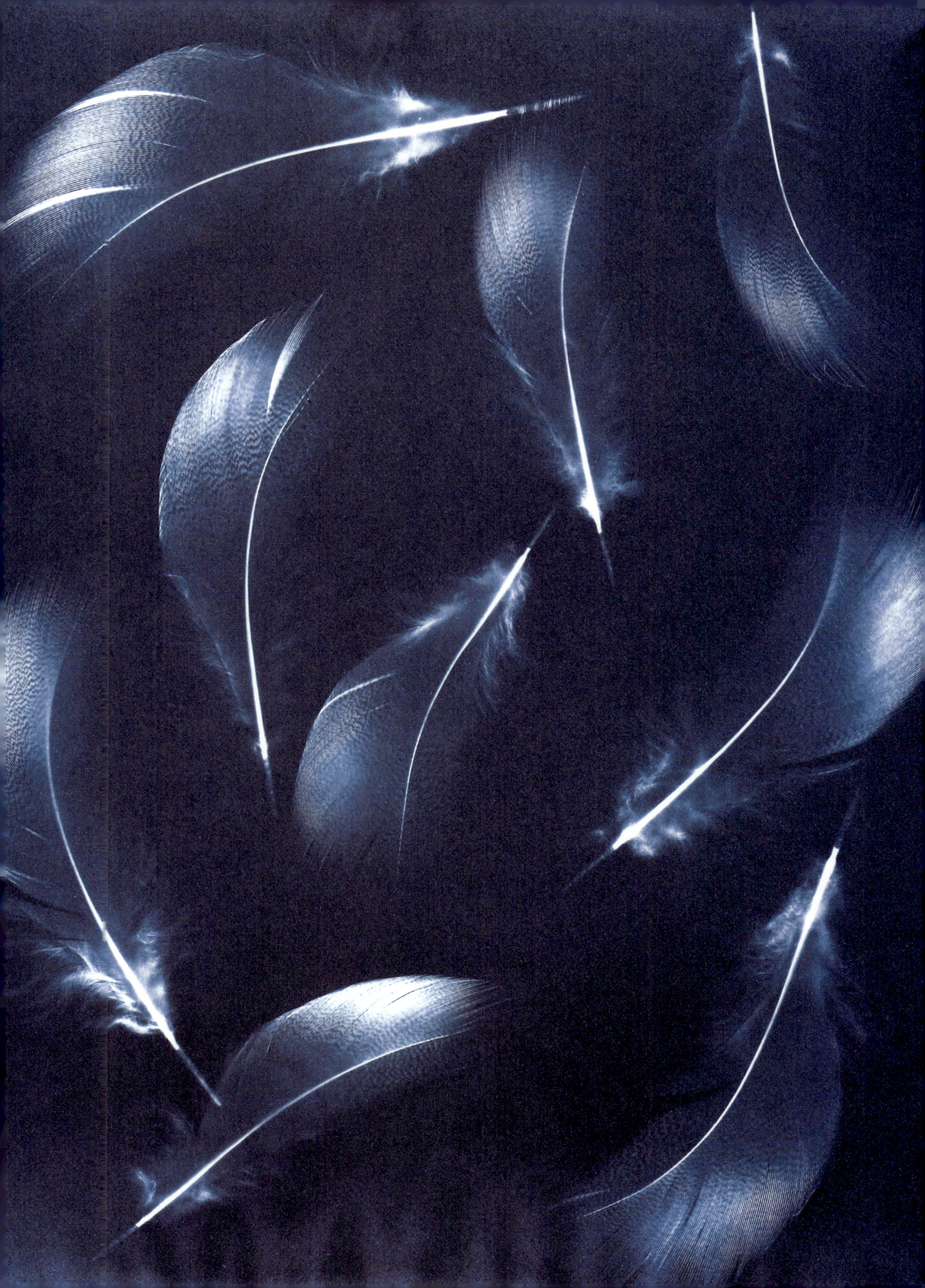

VICTOR SCHRAGER's photographs have been featured in numerous solo and group exhibitions in the United States, Europe, and Japan over the past 20 years. He has received fellowships from The John Simon Guggenheim Foundation, The MacDowell Colony, and The National Endowment for the Arts, and his photographs are included in numerous public and private collections around the world, including The Museum of Modern Art, Whitney Museum of American Art, San Francicso Museum of Modern Art, and Houston Museum of Fine Arts.

A.S. BYATT novels include *Possession* (winner of the Booker Prize in 1990), and the sequence *The Virgin in the Garden, Still Life,* and *Babel Tower*. She has also written two novellas, published together as *Angels and Insects,* and four collections of shorter works, including *The Matisse Stories* and *The Djinn in the Nightingale's Eye*. Her most recent works are the novel *The Biographer's Tale* and a collection of critical writing, *On Histories and Stories*. Educated at Cambridge, she was a senior lecturer at University College, London, before becoming a full-time writer in 1983.

STEPHEN DOYLE leads a New York design studio, Doyle Partners. Their work spans publishing, corporate, packaging, environmental, and motion graphics. His studio's work has received numerous top design awards as well as critical recognition from more than 50 publications for work for Knopf, Harper Collins, Barnes & Noble, Talk Miramax Books, The Museum of Modern Art, and Cooper-Hewitt National Design Museum, among others.

Use of the following material is gratefully acknowledged:

"Never Again Would Birds' Song be the Same" from *The Poetry of Robert Frost,* edited by Edward Connery Lathem, the Estate of Robert Frost and Jonathan Cape as publisher. Copyright 1942 by Robert Frost, © 1970 by Lesley Frost Ballantine, © 1969 by Henry Holt and Co. Used by permission of The Random House Group Limited and Henry Holt and Company, LLC.

Selected quotes from *The Book of Beasts* edited and translated by T.H. White. Copyright © 1984 by T.H. White. Reprinted by permission of The Random House Group.

Selected quotes from *The Works of Geoffrey Chaucer* edited by F.N. Robinson. Copyright © 1957 by F.N. Robinson. Reprinted by permission of Houghton Mifflin Company.

Selected quotes from *Saint Francis: Nature Mystic* by Edward A. Armstrong. Copyright © 1973 by E.A. Armstrong. Reprinted by permission of University of California Press.

Selected quotes from *Selected Journals & Other Writings* by James J. Audubon, edited by Ben Forkner. Copyright © 1996 by Ben Forkner. Published by Penguin Putnam, Inc.

Selected quotes from *The Natural History of Selbourne* by Gilbert White. Published by J.M. Dent.

Selected quotes from *The Origin of Species* by Charles Darwin. Introduction copyright © 1996. Reprinted by permission of Oxford University Press.

Excerpts from *Silent Spring* by Rachel Carson. Copyright © 1962 by Rachel L. Carson, renewed 1990 by Roger Christie. Reprinted by permission of Houghton Mifflin Company, Hamish Hamilton Limited, Laurence Pollinger Limited, and the Estate of Rachel Carson. All rights reserved.

Selected quotes from *Much Depends on Dinner* by Margaret Visser. Copyright © 1986 by Margaret Visser. Reprinted by permission of Grove/Atlantic, Inc. and McClelland and Stewart, Ltd.

Selected quotes from *The Filey Brigg Bird Report.* Reprinted by permission of Filey Brigg Ornithological Group.